BBC

VOLUME 28

JAMES

P9-CSE-308

FIRST and SECOND PETER

FIRST SECOND and THIRD JOHN

and JUDE

Earl S. Johnson, Jr.

ABINGDON PRESS
Nashville

James—Jude

This book is printed on recycled, acid-free paper.

Library of Congress Cataloging-in-Publication Data

Cokesbury basic Bible commentary.
  Basic Bible commentary / by Linda B. Hinton . . . [et al.].
    p. cm.
  Originally published: Cokesbury basic Bible commentary. Nashville: Graded Press, © 1988.
  ISBN 0-687-02620-2 (pbk. : v. 1 : alk. paper)
  1. Bible—Commentaries. I. Hinton, Linda B. II. Title.
[BS491.2.C65 1994]
220.7—dc20   94-10965
                                                                              CIP

ISBN 0-687-02648-2 (v. 28, James–Jude)
ISBN 0-687-02620-2 (v. 1, Genesis)
ISBN 0-687-02621-0 (v. 2, Exodus–Leviticus)
ISBN 0-687-02622-9 (v. 3, Numbers–Deuteronomy)
ISBN 0-687-02623-7 (v. 4, Joshua–Ruth)
ISBN 0-687-02624-5 (v. 5, 1–2 Samuel)
ISBN 0-687-02625-3 (v. 6, 1–2 Kings)
ISBN 0-687-02626-1 (v. 7, 2 Chronicles)
ISBN 0-687-02627-X (v. 8, Ezra–Esther)
ISBN 0-687-02628-8 (v. 9, Job)
ISBN 0-687-02629-6 (v. 10, Psalms)
ISBN 0-687-02630-X (v. 11, Proverbs–Song of Solomon)
ISBN 0-687-02631-8 (v. 12, Isaiah)
ISBN 0-687-02632-6 (v. 13, Jeremiah–Lamentations)
ISBN 0-687-02633-4 (v. 14, Ezekiel–Daniel)
ISBN 0-687-02634-2 (v. 15, Hosea–Jonah)
ISBN 0-687-02635-0 (v. 16, Micah–Malachi)
ISBN 0-687-02636-9 (v. 17, Matthew)
ISBN 0-687-02637-7 (v. 18, Mark)
ISBN 0-687-02638-5 (v. 19, Luke)
ISBN 0-687-02639-3 (v. 20, John)
ISBN 0-687-02640-7 (v. 21, Acts)
ISBN 0-687-02642-3 (v. 22, Romans)
ISBN 0-687-02643-1 (v. 23, 1–2 Corinthians)
ISBN 0-687-02644-X (v. 24, Galatians–Ephesians)
ISBN 0-687-02645-8 (v. 25, Philippians–2 Thessalonians)
ISBN 0-687-02646-6 (v. 26, 1 Timothy–Philemon)
ISBN 0-687-02647-4 (v. 27, Hebrews)
ISBN 0-687-02649-0 (v. 29, Revelation)
ISBN 0-687-02650-4 (complete set of 29 vols.)

99 00 01 02 03—10 9 8 7 6 5 4
MANUFACTURED IN THE UNITED STATES OF AMERICA

Contents

Outline of James through Jude

James

I. Greetings (1:1)
II. Trials and Temptations (1:2-15)
III. God's Gifts and God's Word (1:16-27)
    A. Good gifts from God (1:16-18)
    B. Bad words and the word (1:19-21)
    C. Be doers and not hearers only (1:22-25)
    D. What does it mean to be religious? (1:26-27)
IV. Treating the Poor and the Rich Equally (2:1-13)
V. Faith and Works (2:14-26)
VI. The Tongue Is a Fire (3:1-12)
VII. Jealousy and Pride (3:13–4:17)
    A. True wisdom versus jealousy (3:3-18)
    B. Friendship with the world (4:1-10)
    C. Who are you to judge your neighbor? (4:11-12)
    D. The foolishness of planning ahead (4:13-17)
VIII. Oppressors of the Poor, Beware (5:1-6)
IX. Be Patient, Jesus Is Coming (5:7-11)
X. Concern for the Weaker Members (5:12-20)
    A. Take no oaths (5:12)
    B. Pray for healing (5:13-18)
    C. Correct the backslider (5:19-20)

First Peter

I. Greetings (1:1-2)
II. The Essentials of the Christian Faith (1:3–2:3)
   A. The indestructible faith in Christ (1:3-9)
   B. The witness of the prophets (1:10-12)
   C. Be holy, as he is holy (1:13–2:3)
III. The Living Stone and the Living House (2:4-10)
IV. Good Conduct Removes Alien Status (2:11–3:12)
   A. Set an example to the Gentiles (2:11-12)
   B. Relationships to government (2:13-17)
   C. House servants and masters (2:18-20)
   D. The example of Christ (2:21-25)
   E. Husbands and wives (3:1-7)
   F. Summary (3:8-12)
V. Perspectives on Persecution (3:13–4:19)
VI. Advice to Church Leaders (5:1-11)
VII. Conclusions (5:12-14)

Second Peter

I. Greetings (1:1-2)
II. Knowledge, Virtue, and Calling (1:3-11)
III. Peter's Own Experiences (1:12-21)
IV. The Danger of False Prophets (2:1-22)
V. Is Christ Really Coming Again? (3:1-18)

First John

I. Christ Is From the Beginning (1:1-4)
II. God Is Light (1:5-10)
III. The Nature of Sin (2:1-29)
   A. The danger of sin (2:1-14)
   B. The danger of the world (2:15-17)
   C. The danger of the Antichrist (2:18-29)

Second John

Third John

Jude

Introduction to James

The Nature of James

James is the first of the books of the New Testament that are traditionally referred to as "the Catholic Epistles." "Catholic" means "general" and refers to the fact that most of these letters were written to general audiences rather than specific congregations. Along with 1 and 2 Peter; 1, 2, and 3 John; and Jude, James was written toward the end of the first century A.D. or the beginning of the second century. At that time, the church was establishing itself as an institution and struggling to help its members establish a consistent code of ethics.

Strictly speaking, James is not a letter, since it is not written to any congregation by name. It is not addressed to particular problems as are 1 and 2 Corinthians, Galatians, and Romans. Rather, it deals with general Christian concerns.

Since James is mainly interested in offering its readers Christian advice, it is usually referred to as a homily. The book fits in with a type of literature commonly known in the ancient world as "exhortation" or parenesis. Advice is given in almost all the New Testament letters, but it is usually accompanied by preaching or teaching as well as references to particular problems faced by a church or a group of churches. In James, however, nothing but exhortation is presented as the author discusses several main concerns:

•the danger of double-mindedness (1:8; 4:8),
•the danger of pride (1:9, 21-23; 2:1-7, 13; 3:1; 4:13-17),
•how to endure in a time of trial (1:2-4, 12-15),
•maintaining equality between the rich and the poor (2:1-7, 14-17; 5:1-6),
•hearing and doing (1:22-25; 2:14-26; 4:17),
•the danger of loose talk (1:19; 3:1-12).

Authorship

According to the first verse, the author of the homily is *James, a servant of God and of the Lord Jesus Christ*. The New Testament mentions several different men by that name: James, the brother of Jesus (Mark 6:3); James, the son of Alphaeus, one of Jesus' disciples (Luke 6:15); James, the brother of John, one of the the the sons of Zebedee whom Jesus also called as a disciple (Mark 3:17); James, the father of Judas (not Judas Iscariot; Luke 6:16); James the younger, who was with the women at the cross (Mark 15:40).

Traditionally, it was thought that the author of James was the brother of Jesus who was given the title *James the Just*. Although he was not a disciple during Jesus' lifetime (Mark 3:21, 31-35; John 7:3-5), he became a leading figure in Jerusalem after Jesus' resurrection. Probably he became the head of the church after Peter left on his first missionary tour (Acts 12:17). Paul mentions him in Galatians 1:19 and 2:9 as one of the *pillars* of the church (see Acts 15) and one who may have opposed certain aspects of his ministry (Acts 2:12).

Although it is easy to understand why Christians would want to read something written by the Lord's own brother, most scholars doubt that James was the true author of the epistle of James. Jesus' name is only mentioned twice throughout the whole work (1:1; 2:1) and nothing is said about his relationship to the author. The homily is written in a highly polished Greek style, one which an uneducated fisherman like the brother of

Jesus would not be likely to use. According to the Jewish historian Flavius Josephus, James died in A.D. 62. However, the homily clearly reflects the ideas and concerns of a much later period when Hebrews, Jude, and 1 and 2 Peter were also written. Some scholars think that James may have written parts of the original epistle and that the final draft was composed by someone else who used his name to make sure that it would be widely read. However, it is impossible to be sure who the author was.

For reasons that are not completely clear, James was not fully accepted by the church until the fourth century. Questions about its authorship must have been raised from the start. Some Christians have been suspicious of its value, saying it has very little specific Christian teaching in it. Some scholars have suggested, in fact, that it was originally written by Jews who lived outside of Palestine and was given a few Christian additions by Christian writers so it could be presented as the work of Jesus' brother. Indeed, during the Protestant Reformation, Martin Luther dismissed it as an "epistle of straw," one that was not of primary importance because it was not written by an apostle.

Faith Versus Works

Despite suspicions concerning the value of James, the homily has been of great importance to Christians because it does take up important Christian themes. Scholars note that there are more than thirty-five indirect references to the teaching of Jesus in the epistle, twenty-five of which come from the Sermon on the Mount. The homily also takes up a number of ethical questions that are important in the rest of the New Testament and are significant for believers in any time.

Of particular importance, of course, is the discussion of faith and works that the author carefully develops. Although the apostle Paul argues in Romans 3–4 and

Galatians 2–4 that people are put right with God only through their faith in Jesus Christ and that they cannot earn their salvation by works, the author of James lives in a time when people are content to mouth their beliefs without putting them into practice. It is not enough, he argues, to say that you believe in Jesus Christ, if you are not willing to follow him in the way you live. Christians may be saved by faith, but without the proof of actions and love expressed to one's neighbor in concrete deeds, faith is truly dead.

The Readers

Reference is made in 1:1 to the readers as *the twelve tribes in the Dispersion* (NRSV; NIV = *scattered among the nations*). *Dispersion* is a Jewish term that refers to the fact that the Jewish people lived all over the world, either because they were forced out of Palestine by their enemies or because they chose to live elsewhere. The author probably uses it as a code word for Jewish Christians, but it is impossible to tell where they lived. The church could have been anywhere in the Roman Empire (compare 1 Peter 1:1).

James 1:1

Greetings (1:1)

James starts with a greeting that is similar to that of other letters in the New Testament. In the ancient world most letters began in the same way, with the identification of the writer and his or her credentials, the naming of the person or people who would receive the message, and the greeting. In this case, as was pointed out in the Introduction, the letter format is used to begin a sermon or homily.

The author identifies himself as *James, a servant of God*, but it is not certain who he is (see the Introduction). It is common for New Testament writers to introduce themselves as servants or slaves (the Greek word *doulos* literally means *slave*; see Romans 1:1; Philippians 1:1; Titus 1:1). In the Old Testament, leaders whom God chose for the people are often called servants (Exodus 32:13; Deuteronomy 34:5). In the servant songs (Isaiah 42:1-4; 49:1-6; 50:4-9; 52:13–53:12), the prophet speaks passionately about the messiah who will not be a mighty king but a suffering servant of the Lord. In the New Testament Jesus presents himself as a servant (John 13:1-20) and teaches the disciples that they too must serve others (Mark 9:35; 10:42-45).

Jesus is referred to as *Lord*. *Lord* is a title of honor that was commonly used to refer to a king, an emperor, a landowner, a slavemaster, or an employer. In the Old Testament it is often used as a title for God.

Jesus is considered to be the Lord above all other lords, whether they are emperors or other gods or goddesses (Acts 2:34, 36; 11:20; Philippians 2:11). The first Christians used the prayer *our Lord, come (maranatha)* to describe their faith that Jesus would return in power at the end of history (1 Corinthians 16:22; Revelation 22:20; see also James 5:7-8). The title is used throughout James to describe the authority, power, majesty, and mercy of God in Christ (1:7; 2:1; 3:9; 4:10, 15; 5:4, 10, 14, 15).

James addresses his message to the *twelve tribes in the Dispersion*. For *dispersion* see the Introduction. *The twelve tribes* refers to the twelve tribes of the nation of Israel that were named after the sons of the patriarch Jacob (Genesis 35:22-26; Chapter 49; Deuteronomy 27:12-13; 1 Chronicles 2:1-2). It is difficult to see why James would give Christians such a Jewish title. Some scholars suggest that he wants to emphasize that the church was the New Israel predicted in the Old Testament (Jeremiah 3:18; Ezekiel 37:9-14). Perhaps he uses it as a code to indicate that his readers are all Jewish Christians. It is also possible that, since he is going to be discussing the trials and temptations that Christians face in 1:1-15, he connects his greetings with the well-known tradition that in spite of the temptations it must face, the church will nevertheless be the final judge of the twelve tribes of Israel (Matthew 19:28; Luke 22:28-30; Revelation 7:4-9).

§ § § § § § §

The Message of James 1:1

In this opening verse, James introduces himself and gives initial greetings to his readers. He does not indicate who they are, except to refer to them as *the twelve tribes in the Dispersion*, a title whose meaning is uncertain.

§ § § § § § §

James 1:2-15

Introduction to These Verses

The outline of James's homily is not easy to determine, because even though it contains a number of connected themes, it is not tightly organized. Many of its parts are loosely tied together by the association of similar ideas or words. In 1:2-15, for example, James is mainly concerned to discuss the effects of trials and temptations on the Christian life, although he also introduces here his criticisms of two different types of people within the church—the rich and the double-minded believers.

Trials and Temptations (1:2-15)

James indicates that his readers are facing certain crises in their church (*trials, testing of your faith*), but he discusses them in such general terms that it is difficult to know precisely what they are. Perhaps he only has in mind the kinds of problems that all Christian people encounter as they try to live a Christ-centered life.

He begins this section by saying that Christians should *consider it pure joy* when they face trials and the testing of their faith. James stands within a well-known Christian tradition that refuses to insist that one must be happy, healthy, or wealthy to be joyful. (See Romans 5:2-5 and 1 Peter 1:6-7.) Jesus taught that those who are blessed by God are those who are persecuted for their faith, those who mourn for the sin and suffering in the world (Matthew 5:4, 9, 10).

Similarly, Paul speaks repeatedly about joy and rejoicing in his letter to the Philippians, even though he was miserable and in prison when he wrote it (4:4-5, 10-15). As he says in Romans, *Rejoice in hope, be patient in suffering, persevere in prayer* (Romans 12:12 NRSV). Joy is not a feeling that the Christian conjures up. It is a fruit of the Holy Spirit (Galatians 5:22) that is always available, regardless of circumstances.

James uses two different words to describe the difficult situation faced by his readers: *trials* (verse 2) and *testing* (verse 3). The word *trial* is used in the New Testament to refer to persecution that comes to Christian people as the normal consequence of being believers and witnessing to Christ in a world that rejects him (see 1 Peter 4:12). The word also describes temptations and the enticements of sin that disturb faith (Matthew 6:13; 26:41; Luke 8:13; 1 Peter 1:6; 2 Peter 2:9). *Testing* describes the means by which believers have their faith challenged or examined (see 2 Corinthians 13:5; Galatians 6:4).

James makes clear in verses 13-15 that he does not agree with those who think that God sends trials and temptations to test faith (see 2 Thessalonians 1:4). James is not an admirer of the kind of thinking found in Job, where it is asserted that God would do anything, even give Satan a free hand, to test persons' faith. God, James says, has nothing to do with evil, and would never use it to accomplish good purposes. This should be good news for Christians who often lose their faith when tragedy strikes because they think that God is punishing them for some reason. "Do not think that God would treat you in such an unloving way," James argues. As Paul points out in 1 Corinthians 10:13, even though God does not send evil, God can use it once it arrives to make good things happen. The Christian must be faithful and trust in God's goodness.

James outlines the good results that can be expected from trials. They include *perseverance* (NIV; NRSV =

14

endurance, verses 3-4), perfection and completion (verse 4), and *the crown of life* (verse 12). Perseverance is the endurance and the courage that God gives to those who are suffering (Luke 21:19; 2 Corinthians 1:6; 6:4; 1 Thessalonians 2:1-2; 2 Timothy 3:10). Steadfastness leads the believer to hope in the future (2 Thessalonians 1:4); it is a characteristic of Christ himself (2 Thessalonians 3:5).

It is difficult to know what the words *that you may be mature and complete, lacking in nothing* (verse 4) mean. In Jewish tradition it was believed that people could become perfect, that is, live without sin, if they could keep the law in every way (see Leviticus 18:5). The people who lived at Qumran, at the northern end of the Dead Sea, also believed that if they could remain morally and ritually pure they could become "perfect of way." The apostle Paul vigorously denies that such a thing is possible, however, and says that the law only leads to sin (Romans 2:12; 3:9; Galatians 3:10-14).

Possibly James is looking ahead in Christian hope, knowing that Christians hover between sin and perfection. They are not yet made whole in Christ, but look forward to that time when Christ, through his love, will make all those who believe in him perfect, just as he is perfect (see Hebrews 2:10; 7:19, 28; 10:1; 11:40; 12:23; 1 John 2:5; 4:12, 18).

Verses 5-8 introduce another major theme as James refers to the *double-minded* person who wavers in faith. Although he has made it clear already that Christians will be faced with trials and temptations, James asserts that the true believer will not succumb to them. *Double-minded* is a literal translation of the Greek word that refers to someone who is thinking or looking two ways at once. It refers to a faith that is wavering and hesitating. James uses the same word again in 4:8 to describe those who are yielding to evil passions, those who are far away from God. Double-minded people, as the rest of the homily points out, are those who try to maintain their faith while giving in at the same time to wealth and property. They are believers who want to talk about faith but do not want to help their neighbors. Christians must be single-minded in their devotion to Christ if they want to remain spiritually alive (5:20).

In verses 9-11 James introduces a theme that is of particular significance to him—the fact that Christians must not be tempted by wealth. They must remain humble if they want to retain the crown of eternal life. He will discuss this theme more fully in 1:27; 2:1-7; and 5:1-6. See the discussions there. Verse 11 is an allusion to Old Testament ideas, either from Isaiah 40:6-8 or Psalm 102:4, 11.

Crown of life (verse 12) refers to the headpieces worn by royalty, priests, and other people in special positions of honor. The early Christians believed that they would receive such a crown as the final reward for the steadfastness of their faith (2 Timothy 4:8; 1 Peter 5:4; Revelation 2:10).

§ § § § § § §

The Message of James 1:2-15

In the first section the author of James indicates that his readers are suffering from trials and temptations that besiege Christians as they try to live a Christian life in the midst of an evil world. Although these trials are not sent by God in any way, they will produce endurance and courage, qualities that will eventually lead to Christian perfection.

The Christian must not be double-minded but must be single-minded in devotion to Christ and his example, remaining humble and not tempted by wealth.

§ § § § § § §

Introduction to These Verses

In this section James continues and expands the arguments that he began in 1:5 and 1:13. Here is an outline of this section.
  I. Good Gifts from God (1:16-18)
  II. Bad Words and the Word (1:19-21)
  III. Be Doers and Not Hearers Only (1:22-25)
  IV. What Does It Mean to Be Religious? (1:26-27)

Good Gifts from God (1:16-18)
The Christian reader should not doubt God's wisdom and goodness no matter what happens. God does not bring evil or temptation but only gives good gifts.

In this section the author uses a style that was often found in a type of writing known as a diatribe. A diatribe was well-known in the ancient world as a composition written to argue against and refute opponents. Warnings are given to the reader to be careful as in 1:16 (see also 1 Corinthians 6:9; 15:33; Galatians 6:7); objections that imaginary opponents might raise are dispensed with (2:18); enemies are called names (1:8; 2:20; 4:4); people who are not present are ridiculed (4:13; 5:1); and rhetorical questions are repeatedly asked (2:2-4, 7, 14-16; 3:11-12, 13; 4:1).

Verses 16-17 raise the possibility that believers might be tricked into believing a lie (see 5:19-20), that is, accepting the notion that evil things come from God.

Actually, just the opposite is the case, because all good things come from God who never changes and is always good.

Bible scholars recognize that the words *every good and perfect gift is from above* (NIV) are from a proverb well-known in the ancient world. The saying probably originally meant something like "all things are good in some way" or "don't look a gift horse in the mouth." James uses the saying in a Christian sense to mean that God is the giver of gifts to believers. Christians believe that God's gift is seen mainly in the person of Jesus Christ (John 4:10), in the forgiveness of sins (Romans 5:15, 17; 2 Corinthians 9:15; Ephesians 3:7; 4:7; Hebrews 6:4), and in the presence of the Holy Spirit (Acts 2:38; 8:20; 10:45; 11:17).

The clause *coming down from the Father of lights with whom there is no variation or shadow due to change* (NRSV) refers to God's creation of the light and the stars (Genesis 1:14-18; Psalm 136:7; Jeremiah 31:35) and to the fact that the true light came in Jesus Christ, God's Son. Those who do not believe in Christ are lost in the darkness of sin (Ephesians 4:18), whereas those who are in Christ are illuminated by the one who is himself the light of the world (Luke 1:79; 2:32; John 1:5; 3:19; 8:12; 9:5; 12:35; Colossians 1:12-14; 1 John 1:5-7; 2:8).

No variation or shadow of change may be an argument against those who believed in astrology. For James, life is not determined by the position of the stars or solar or lunar eclipses. God is the true light who never has any shadows at all.

In verse 18 James changes metaphors and uses a feminine image of giving birth (*he gave us birth by the word of truth*) to indicate that God makes believers children of God through the preached and written word. Although modern readers are not used to thinking of God as "mother," it is not an uncommon way to describe divine activity in the Bible (see Numbers 11:12;

Deuteronomy 32:18; Psalm 22:9; 90:2; Isaiah 66:13; Luke 13:34; Galatians 4:19). No doubt James has the idea of the new birth in Christ in mind here (John 1:13; 3:3-8; 1 Corinthians 4:15; Ephesians 1:5; Titus 3:5; 1 Peter 1:3, 23; 1 John 3:9; 4:10).

First fruits is a reference to the biblical idea that fruits that ripened first were very tasty and special and were a guarantee of a good harvest. They were given to God as an offering by the nation at the feast of Weeks (Leviticus 23:10) or by individuals (Exodus 23:19; Deuteronomy 26:1-11).

In the New Testament *first fruits* refers to gifts given to believers by the Holy Spirit (Romans 8:23). First fruits can also be the Christians themselves as the first harvest of Christ's work (Romans 16:5) or his resurrection (1 Corinthians 15:20, 23). Probably James sees his readers as the guarantee that people all over the world will turn to Christ through the preaching of the word of truth.

Bad Words and the Word (1:19-21)

The emphasis switches in verses 19-21 from God's word to human words. Christians must hear God's word, but they must also be careful how they speak themselves. Proverbial sayings about discretion in speech and the danger of loose talk were well-known in the ancient world (see Proverbs 5:1-2; 10:18-21; 13:3; 29:20). James will say much more about the danger of a loose tongue in 1:26 and 3:1-12. See the discussions there.

Warnings about the inappropriateness of expressing anger were also common (Psalm 4:4; Proverbs 15:1; Ephesians 4:26-27). James indicates that anger will prevent the believer from achieving righteousness, that is, the forgiveness of sin that God makes possible through Christ (see Matthew 5:6, 20; 6:33; Romans 1:17). Anger does not reflect the kind of justice God expects the people to give to others (1:27; 2:1-9; Ephesians 4:31;

Colossians 3:8). Enmity and hatred can keep people out of the kingdom of God (Galatians 5:19-21).

Moral Filth (NIV; NRSV = *sordidness,* verse 21) refers to language spiced with vulgarity and sexual innuendo. It is not the way Christians should speak (see Luke 6:45; Ephesians 4:29; 5:4). *Meekness* (NRSV; NIV = *humbly*) comes from the same Greek word that is translated *meek* in Matthew 5:5, *blessed are the meek.* In the ancient world, *meek* had the meaning *tamed,* and often referred to wild horses that had been trained. The same idea is found in Matthew 11:29, where Jesus speaks metaphorically of the taming of an ox: Under Christ a wild beast becomes domesticated and can become gentle and lowly of heart, fit for God's service. (See also Galatians 6:1; 2 Corinthians 10:1; Ephesians 4:2; Colossians 3:12; Titus 3:2; 1 Peter 3:15.)

The implanted word indicates that when Christians hear God's word it is planted in them like a seed. Christian teachers plant the word in the hearts of believers and they become God's field (1 Corinthians 3:6-9). Jesus warns that they must be very careful because the seed/word can easily be choked out by all kinds of temptations and distractions (Mark 4:1-20).

Be Doers and Not Hearers Only (1:22-25)

Verse 22 is one of the main keynotes of James's message to his Christian readers. It is one which will be repeated over and over again throughout the letter (2:2-4, 12, 14, 17, 24, 26). It is summed up in 2:17, where James indicates that if one does nothing more than hear God's word and does not act upon it, then his or her faith is non-productive and dead in the ground. Common sense and the Scriptures support James's warning: Clearly, a person who says one thing and does another is not a true believer. See Deuteronomy 28:58; 29:29; Matthew 7:12, 24-27; Luke 3:8; Acts 5:1-11; 7:53; Galatians 2:11-18; 6:2

for a few references to the important connection between doing and believing.

In verses 23-24 James compares the activities of the hearer who does nothing to a man who looks in a mirror and then forgets what he looks like. Mirrors were commonplace in the first century, and James observes that a man might study his face to comb his hair or shave in the morning but forget what he really looks like before much time passes. The Greek word he uses for *face* (NIV; NRSV = *themselves*) is *genesis*. It refers not only to one's physical looks but also to one's essence or existence, who one really is. Persons who do not do the word of God are like persons who do not really know who they are. They lack the most essential elements for discerning spiritual truth and knowing what life is really about.

If they look into the *perfect law*, however, they will see a reflection not only of what they are physically, but also of what they can become spiritually. By *law* James means the law of God that is found in the Ten Commandments and the Old Testament (see Psalm 19:7; 119) and is fulfilled in Jesus Christ.

Although Paul at times argues that the law cannot bring life but only death (Romans 2:12; 3:19-20; 7:7-23; Galatians 3:10), James seems to have a much more positive attitude toward its function in God's plan. Perhaps James is thinking more along the lines of the teaching of Jesus in Matthew 5:17 when he says that he did not come to abolish the law but to fulfill it. When Paul is thinking more positively about his Jewish background, he also admits that the law served a good function (Galatians 4:23-29) and that in Christ the Christian can complete God's original plan for salvation (Romans 3:31; Galatians 3:21-22).

It is difficult to know for certain, nevertheless, what James means by the expression the *law of liberty* (NRSV; NIV = *law that gives freedom*, see 2:12). Paul thinks that freedom comes chiefly through the action of the Holy Spirit (Galatians 5:1, 13-14, 16-26), but James does not mention the Spirit. Probably he is not thinking very deeply here about the law's role in history, but is simply asserting that if one follows God's plan for right action then one is truly free.

What Does It Mean to Be Religious? (1:26-27)

Here James defines pure and undefiled religion. The word *religion* is used only here in the whole New Testament, and the verb "to be religious" is found only in Acts 26:5 and Colossians 2:18. Both words refer to the worship of God and the practice of religion. Here James returns to the teachings of the Old Testament and argues that true religion is to obey God's directive to take care of widows and orphans (Deuteronomy 14:29; 24:17-22; Jeremiah 5:28; Ezekiel 22:7; Zechariah 7:10) and to keep oneself ritually and spiritually clean. Both ideas are found in the New Testament as well (Acts 6:1-6; 1 Timothy 5:3-16; 1 Peter 1:19; 2 Peter 3:14), and in 2:8 James will directly connect the command to help the poor with Jesus' teaching about the law of love.

§ § § § § § §

The Message of James 1:16-27

In the second half of the first chapter James introduces some of the major themes of his homily. Christians must realize that God has nothing but good gifts for us. God is a God of light, and so illumines believers with God's word.

The believer must not only hear God's word but must be careful how she or speaks as well. Filthy and angry talk is not appropriate for Christians. It separates them from the righteousness of God.

Christians must do more than hear God's word. They must act out their faith as well. Those who do not put their faith into action are not being true to themselves or to the Scriptures.

§ § § § § § §

James 2:1-13

Introduction to These Verses

In chapter 2 James identifies a serious lack of Christian fellowship in the church communities to which he is writing. When people come to church dinners they do not observe the equality that Christ's forgiveness brings. If the apostle Paul can write that *There is neither Jew nor Greek, slave nor free, male nor female; for you are all one in Christ Jesus* (Galatians 3:28), James observes that there are those who clearly believe that some Christians are more "equal" than others. The situation is one that is very easy to understand. When the churches met for fellowship dinners or to celebrate the Lord's Supper, preference was shown to the rich and the famous. They were given seats of special honor, just the kind of seats that Jesus said would not be awarded in his kingdom (Mark 10:37-40), and the poor were put in positions of disgrace. In verse 5 James may be referring to Jesus' teaching in the Beatitudes. There Jesus reminds persons that they cannot treat the poor that way because God has chosen the poor in the world to be rich in faith and heirs of the Kingdom (Matthew 5:3; Luke 6:20, 24-25).

Treating the Poor and the Rich Equally (2:1-13)

The situation James describes here is quite similar to two incidents that Paul reports. In 1 Corinthians 11:17-34 Paul indicates that the Corinthians are finding that some people are sick and dying because they are not observing the Lord's Supper correctly. The rich people are coming in early, and at the church dinner they eat their fine food without waiting for the poorer, working class members to arrive. These divisions in the assembly have profaned the body and blood of the Lord (verse 27), and until they are corrected the congregation will not be able to worship together properly. See also Galatians 2:11-14 for the description of another time when the presence of Christ at a Christian table was dishonored.

Table fellowship is critical to Christians, and because of the Lord's Supper it reminds believers that Christ died for all so that all could be accepted as forgiven children by God. If people deny the poor equality at Christ's table, they deny Christ too (Matthew 25:31-46).

Helping the poor is an imperative that Christians inherited from the teachings of the Old Testament. The Jewish law had special provisions in it to make sure that those who were economically at the bottom of the ladder would be protected. Attention was to be paid to slaves, strangers, widows, orphans, and the poor as part of God's command (Exodus 22:21-27; 23:10-11). God is the God of the poor. God will hear their cries and help them (see Genesis 15:12-14; Leviticus 25:10-24; Deuteronomy 15:11-18; Psalm 72:12-14).

In other passages in the New Testament the concern for the poor is also emphasized by Jesus and those who follow him. In his inaugural sermon Jesus says that he has come to preach good news to the poor and set the oppressed at liberty (Luke 4:16-30). His disciples are ordered to leave behind all material goods (Mark 6:6-11), and they are not to be attached to property if they want to avoid being separated from God (Mark 1:16-21; 10:17-30; Luke 9:59-62; 16:19-31).

The first believers took Jesus' teaching literally as they gave away their lands and goods to help the poor. The Jerusalem Christians shared everything they had (Acts 4:32) and distributed these goods to anyone in need (Acts

2:42-46). Acts 21:10-16 indicates that it was Paul's eagerness to collect money for the impoverished and hungry church in Jerusalem that eventually led to his arrest and martyrdom in Rome. In verse 7 James indicates that the denial of this tradition, by exploitation of the poor, is a serious offense. Since it is so centrally connected with what Jesus taught and was as a person, any Christian who ignores the poor blasphemes Jesus' name and is in danger of losing his or her inheritance as a child of God (see Mark 3:28-30; Luke 16:19-31). James will have more to say about the ministry to the poor in 2:15-16 and 5:1-6.

James reminds his readers in verse 8 that equal treatment of Christian brothers and sisters follows Jesus' *royal law* of love, often referred to as the "Golden Rule" (Matthew 22:36-40; Romans 13:9; Galatians 5:14-15). It is called the *royal* law, no doubt, because Jesus continually preached about the kingdom of God and because by the time the letter of James was written Christians were also speaking of the kingdom of Christ (Ephesians 5:5).

The kind of love James means specifically is agape love, self-giving love, generous love, love that is unlimited and willing to sacrifice for the other person. Love is freedom in essence because it lets the self go and is directed only to God and to the other. Agape love is the kind of love that Jesus gave to humanity through his death and resurrection. By following his example Christians can really be free. Love is the first fruit of the Spirit (Galatians 5:22); it is the best gift of the Spirit (1 Corinthians 13:13). Love is the more excellent way. Agape love was such an important thing to the first Christians that it is mentioned more than one hundred times in the New Testament.

In verses 9-11 James discusses more fully his understanding of the Jewish law (see the discussion of James 1:23-25). Here he agrees with the sentiments of Paul, that the law is very difficult, if not impossible, to keep (see Romans 3:9-20, especially verse 20; 3:23-24; 7:4-25;

Galatians 2:16; 3:3, 11-14). It is not possible to fulfill the law in a partial way, or to be somewhat saved. The law must be kept in all of its aspects if it is to lead to salvation.

James does not carry the argument to the same conclusion that Paul reached, however. Paul agrees that the law must be kept wholly to achieve salvation; thus the law cannot save and the believer is totally dependent on faith in Christ. James takes the discussion in a different direction and concludes that since the law is so hard to keep, the Christian must work that much harder not to break it in any way (verses 11-12).

James concludes the section with a warning that Christians will be judged by the same measure by which they judge others. Similar ideas are found in the Lord's Prayer (Matthew 6:12-14; Luke 6:27-32) and the teachings of Paul (Romans 2:6-7). Also see Matthew 5:7; Mark 11:25.

§ § § § § § §

The Message of James 2:1-13

In his fourth section James pinpoints a serious problem that exists in the churches to which he writes. Some of them have forgotten the teaching in the Old Testament and the witness of Jesus that the poor are to receive a special place of honor in God's kingdom. Instead of observing this teaching, some Christians are giving the rich special places in the church and thus denying the oneness of the body of Christ and the fellowship that Jesus' love brings.

In verses 8-13 James reminds his readers that to break the Jewish law in any way means that it is broken in all ways. James advises them to make sure, therefore, that they do not violate the law at all.

§ § § § § § §

James 2:14-26

Introduction to These Verses

This section of James has correctly been seen throughout Christian history as critical for a proper understanding of the author's message. On a superficial level it is easy to comprehend and few Christians would take issue with it. James argues very convincingly that anyone who professes to have faith in Jesus Christ should follow him not only in beliefs but also in actions. Just because people say (verse 14) that they have faith does not mean that they do have it. The proof is in the doing. "Show me your activities," James says in verse 18, "and then I shall really see your faith."

Faith and Works (2:14-26)

People do not have to be Jews or Christians or have the witness of the Scriptures to know that it is hypocritical to say one thing and do something totally opposite. Even non-Christians or atheists should be shocked if a person who professes to follow Jesus by being willing to help the poor actually turns poor people away when they ask for help. James's example in verses 15-16 is similar to some of Jesus' parables, especially the story about the rich man and Lazarus in Luke 16:19-31. Jesus' point is very clear. If a person with financial means passes by the poor day after day without any regard for their hunger, homelessness, or health, then that rich person is spiritually dead (verses 17, 26), is *barren* (NRSV; NIV =

useless, verse 20), is good for nothing, and is totally non-productive.

By arguing in such a way, James puts himself in the company of many other New Testament writers who insist that the evidence of faith is in actions (Matthew 7:7-12; 25:31-46; Romans 2:6-7; 3:9-20; 1 Corinthians 13:2; Ephesians 4:17–5:20; Colossians 3:5-17).

On a deeper level, understanding James 2:14-26 is a little more difficult, especially when what is written there is compared with Paul's perspective of the law in Romans 3–4 and Galatians 2–4. See the Introduction on pages 7-10. Throughout Christian history commentators have struggled with the contrast between Paul's insistence that the works of the law cannot bring salvation no matter how good people are, and James's argument that faith cannot save without works. Many scholars argue that the two authors have a different definition of law or that because they lived in different times they were free to say slightly different things about the same faith.

Paul and James may not have been as far apart as some persons think, but it is dangerous to deny the possibility that biblical passages can contradict each other. Assuming the Bible to contain no contradictory statements does not permit writers coming out of varied situations to have different understandings of the Christian faith. It also fails to acknowledge the possibility that biblical writers may have been in dialogue with one another, sometimes agreeing and sometimes disagreeing, just as Christians converse with each other today.

The contrast between the theology of James and Paul is especially evident in their understanding of the example of Abraham. Biblical writers used Abraham to illustrate the nature of the Christian faith because he was the parent of the Jewish religion. They knew that if they could prove their case about faith by referring to him their readers would be convinced that it had been God's plan from the beginning. Throughout Jewish tradition Abraham was a very important figure, as references in the New Testament show (Matthew 1:1, 2, 17; 3:9; Luke 16:22-30; John 8:39, 53, 58; Acts 7:2-8; Hebrews 7:1-10; 11:8; 1 Peter 3:6). His story is found in the Old Testament in Genesis 12–25.

In Romans 4 Paul uses Abraham to demonstrate that God's plan from the beginning was to save the people by faith, not by works of the law. The promise to Abraham and his descendants, that they should inherit the world, did not come through the law but through the righteousness of faith (verse 13). In Galatians 3–4 Paul argues similarly. The birth of a son, Isaac, to Abraham and Sarah, proves that inheritance is only by faith, not by the works of the law (Galatians 4:21-31).

James, on the other hand, uses the example of Abraham and Isaac to prove just the opposite point. When Abraham was willing to sacrifice his son to God (Genesis 22:9-10), his action showed that he was justified by his works. If he had not been willing to do that, his faith would have been dead. Abraham's belief (James 2:23) was not just a matter of faith but of action. Thus it is clear to James that people are not put right with God by *faith alone* (verse 24).

James concludes with a second illustration to make the same point, the example of Rahab. Jewish tradition often comments favorably on her decision to shelter the spies from Joshua in Jericho and enable them to escape and bring information to his army (Joshua 2). When Joshua destroyed the city, she and her family were saved and permitted to live (Joshua 6:25). In Hebrews 11:31 and 1 Clement 12:1-8, her actions are cited as an example of the power of faith. In James's view, what she did is a testimonial to the fact that people are saved by works.

§ § § § § § §

The Message of James 2:14-26

James 2:14-26 is important for a correct understanding of the author's homily. James knows that it takes more than a statement of belief to make one a believer. Faith must also be backed up by action. People who do not live the Christian faith show that they they do not really believe in Jesus Christ. Faith without works is dead.

James goes farther, however, when he also argues that people cannot be saved by faith alone. He appears to be in serious conflict with the apostle Paul's major assertion in Romans 4 and Galatians 3–4 that salvation is only by faith. The two authors use the example of Abraham in very different ways, Paul showing that he illustrates the fact that salvation is not through works and James demonstrating that it is.

§ § § § § § §

James 3:1-12

Introduction to These Verses

Chapter 3 provides advice for church leaders, especially those who are teachers (3:1, 13), by linking together several proverbial sayings that were well-known in the ancient world.

Teaching was important in the church because it was the way persons became Christians and were taught how they should live in order to follow Christ. Jesus was called a teacher (Mark 4:38; 5:35; 9:17, 38; 13:1; Luke 6:40; John 11:28; 20:16), and the ability to teach was considered to be a gift of the Holy Spirit (1 Corinthians 12:28-29; Colossians 3:16; 1 Timothy 5:17; 2 Timothy 3:16). The first Christians had to be careful because there were people who tried to deceive them through false teaching (1 Timothy 6:3; 2 Timothy 4:3; 1 John 2:26; Jude 4).

The Tongue Is a Fire (3:1-12)

When James says in verse 1 that teachers will be judged with more strictness he reminds his readers that teachers have to be very careful what they say. Since they will influence the faith, thoughts, and actions of young people and new Christians they have a special responsibility and will be held accountable. (See Mark 9:42; 1 Corinthians 3:12-15; 9:27.)

James indicates that he considers himself to be a teacher who falls under his own warning when he writes *we who teach* and *we all stumble in many ways* (NIV; NRSV

= *we all make many mistakes*). To avoid coming under judgment, Christian teachers must be mature in their faith and avoid sin (the literal meaning of *mistakes*). In these verses James especially links the danger of false teaching with the function of the tongue. He has already warned his readers of the danger of loose talk in 1:26 and 2:7. Since a teacher has to speak in order for anyone to learn anything, Christians have to be aware that the tongue is a powerful instrument that can be used for good or evil, building up or tearing down.

Here James builds on Old Testament imagery when he says that the tongue must be bridled because it is a wild and dangerous part of the human body, because it can be as destructive as fire. See Psalms 5:9; 34;13; 39:1; 52:2; 120:3-4; Proverbs 10:20, 31; 12:18; 25:15; Jeremiah 9:5, 8; also Matthew 12:33-37.

In addition to referring to the tongue as a fire, James also says that it is set on fire by *hell*. The Greek word for Hell is *Gehenna*, taken from the Hebrew word that refers to the Valley of Hinnom near Jerusalem in the Kidron Valley. This valley formed part of the boundary between two of the tribes of Israel (Joshua 15:8; 18:16; Nehemiah 11:30). Later it was an infamous place where at least one of the kings of Judah practiced human sacrifice by fire (2 Chronicles 28:3; 33:6; Jeremiah 7:31; 32:35). Jeremiah spoke of its ultimate destruction (Jeremiah 7:32; 19:6), and because of its association with evil religious practices it became known as the fiery place where final judgment would take place on the day of the Lord (Matthew 5:22, 29-30; 13:42, 50; 23:33; 25:41; Mark 9:43-45; Luke 12:5). Later Gehenna became associated with the dwelling place of Satan. James implies that from there comes the fiery, destructive power of the tongue (verse 6).

The unusual phrase *cycle of nature* (NRSV, NIV = *the whole course of his life*) in verse 6 can also be translated *wheel of birth* (see the NRSV note). Since the word in Greek can refer to the wheel of a wagon, a potter's wheel, or even a race track, the expression might also mean the wheel of existence, the cycle of being, or even the race course of life.

In verses 6-10 James continues to refer to the tongue in negative ways when he calls it a *world of evil* (NIV; NRSV = *of iniquity*, verse 6), a *restless evil full of deadly poison* (verse 8), and an instrument used for *cursing* (verse 10). In verse 6 *world of evil* is an unusual expression and could literally be translated *the cosmos of injustice*. Although it is not easy to interpret, the phrase appears to refer to the world of human society that is dominated by evil and sin, the world described in 1 John 5:19 as being under the power of the evil one. In James's view, the tongue, when used incorrectly, can become an instrument of evil, infecting and staining or corrupting the whole person.

The word *restless* (verse 8) in the expression *restless evil* is the same adjective used in 1:8 to describe a person who is double-minded. As one is unstable in all ways, so one's tongue that is not bridled leads to disorder (3:6) and disaster. *Poison* is probably a reference to Old Testament imagery that compares the tongues of enemies to those of deadly serpents (Psalm 58:4-5; 140:3). Whether James is thinking of the serpent's temptation in the story of the garden of Eden (Genesis 3:1-15), is difficult to say.

In verses 9-10 James marvels that one organ, the tongue, can be used for entirely different purposes. It can be used to bless God or curse other people. For the meaning of *bless* (NRSV; NIV = *praise*) see the discussion of 1 Peter 1:3. Examples of curses put on others are also common in the Scriptures (see Genesis 9:25; 49:7; Judges 5:23; 9:20; Proverbs 11:26; 26:2; 1 Corinthians 5:2, 5; Galatians 1:9). James believes that curses are inappropriate coming from the mouths of Christians (see Jude 8-10).

James explores the alternative to having a tongue that causes pain and destruction in the church or the world by referring to ideas that were common throughout Greek and Roman literature. The way to prevent the tongue from doing damage is to have it under control, to have it bridled (verses 2-3) or guided (verse 4). The wild, undisciplined tongue can be controlled just as a horse can be maneuvered by a bit and bridle. Similarly, a large vessel like a boat can be directed, even in the midst of a storm, if the pilot knows how to use a rudder. In the New Testament and early Christian literature, the boat was a symbol for the church (Mark 4:35-41; 6:45-52; 1 Peter 3:20). Tongues that teach and preach have to be controlled to benefit the Christian community when it encounters the storms of faith and persecution.

In verses 11 and 12 James returns to his concept that faith without works is dead. If a spring has clean water in it, it will not provide water that is good to drink and salty at the same time. Similarly, a fig tree cannot produce olives or a grapevine figs. Just as what a well or a tree produces shows what it really is like, so a Christian's activities and language demonstrate what is truly inside. If people are good, their speech and actions will also be good; if they are sinners, the fruit they produce will be bad (see Matthew 7:15-20; 12:33-37).

§ § § § § § §

The Message of James 3:1-12

James 3:1-12 warns Christian readers of the grave responsibilities of being a teacher. Since teachers can influence children and new Christians, they will be judged with greater strictness. James also warns Christians to beware of the power of the tongue. Although it is only a small organ, it can ruin the whole body and do damage to the church. The tongue has to be controlled so that the individual and the congregation can produce the good results that are expected from them.

§ § § § § § §

Introduction to These Chapters

In this section James examines the danger inherent in jealousy and pride.

True Wisdom Versus Jealousy (3:13-18)

Here James contrasts true wisdom, the wisdom *from above* (NRSV; NIV = *from heaven*, 3:15, 17), to the wisdom that is *earthly* (verse 15). Wisdom is a gift of God's Spirit (1 Corinthians 12:8; 2 Peter 3:15), but it is also something that can be lacking in the Christian life (James 1:5). For both Jews and Christians wisdom was a very important part of spiritual life. Certain parts of the Old Testament and the Apocrypha are referred to as Wisdom Literature because the concept of wisdom is so central in them (Job; Proverbs; Ecclesiastes; Wisdom of Jesus ben Sirach; Wisdom of Solomon). In some passages, wisdom is described almost as if "she" were a living person or an extension of God (Proverbs 1:1-6; 2–4; 8–9).

For James, wisdom, like other aspects of faith, has to be nurtured and demonstrated in deeds and actions (verse 17). "Show it," James says, "if you want people to know that you have God's wisdom."

James also warns his readers that there is another kind of wisdom that must be avoided at all costs since it is not from God but is *earthly, unspiritual,* and devilish (verse 15). Probably he is thinking along lines similar to those found in Paul's letters to the Corinthians where Paul teaches that the foolishness of God is stronger than the wisdom of this world (1 Corinthians 1:17-18, 20, 24-25, 27; 2:6; 2 Corinthians 1:12). *Earthly* refers to wisdom that is not from above, not from heaven, not from God, and is therefore inferior (see John 3:12; 1 Corinthians 15:40; 2 Corinthians 5:1). *Unspiritual* means those attitudes and thoughts that have nothing to do with God's Holy Spirit or the fruits of the Spirit (verse 17). *Devilish* implies that those who have wisdom that is not from above have it from below; they derive it from Hell (3:6). Such people must be avoided, just as the devil who inspires them must be resisted (4:7).

In verses 14 and 16 James lists the kinds of vices that are connected with the wisdom from below. They include *envy, selfish ambition,* boasting, lying, *disorder* and *every evil practice* (NIV; NRSV = *wickedness of every kind*). The Greek word for *envy* is probably better translated *zeal* here (see John 2:17; Romans 10:2; 2 Corinthians 12:20; Galatians 5:20; Philippians 3:6). James may have in mind the kind of misdirected zeal that leads to rebellion, anger, or violence. *Selfish ambition* is mentioned twice, in verse 14 and verse 16. In Greek it can also mean *strife* or *contentiousness*, especially in the seeking of political office. It clearly has that meaning in Romans 2:8 *(factious)*, Philippians 1:17 *(partisanship)*, and possibly in Galatians 5:20 where Paul warns against those who seek power in the church.

The *disorder* James mentions in verse 16 refers back to the conditions he describes in 1:8 where he condemns the double-minded person who is unstable, and it also refers to the *restless evil* in 3:8. Those who oppose the truth of the wisdom from above destroy peace in the church.

In contrast to the vices listed in verses 14-16, James describes the virtues that come from the wisdom God gives (verses 17-18). Their main characteristic is a peaceable nature, which is provided by those who make peace. Perhaps James is recalling Jesus' blessing of the peacemakers here (Matthew 5:9), recognizing that peace is the opposite of misdirected zeal and party spirit.

Peace is a gift of God (Leviticus 26:6; 1 Kings 2:33; Psalms 29:11; 85:8; Isaiah 26:12). Christ destroys the enmity that exists between God and humanity and among human beings through his death on the cross (Romans 5:16; Galatians 6:16). Peace is a weapon against the machinations of the devil (Ephesians 6:15). It is something believers should strive for (1 Peter 3:10-12). It is a fruit (see James 3:17) of the Spirit (Galatians 5:22).

Friendship with the World (4:1-10)

This section is loosely connected with 3:13-18 by the catchwords *peace* (3:18) and wars (4:1). Here James discusses three things in the Christian life that cause hostility: war within the individual Christian's heart, fighting between church members, and *enmity* (NRSV; NIV = *hatred*, verse 4) *with God*. Although commentators have debated whether the words *wars, fighting, kill, enmity* and *enemy* are to be taken literally, it is likely that they are all used symbolically by James to indicate the great danger of sin and the way it can lead to spiritual death (see 2:17, 26, faith apart from works is dead; see also Romans 6:1-11; Ephesians 2:1). These words also refer to the infighting in the church that he condemns in 3:14-16.

Possibly James has in mind the first stories in Genesis about Adam and Eve that show how rebellion against God leads to inner turmoil (Genesis 3:8-13), hostility between human beings and God (3:15-19), spiritual and physical death (3:24), and continuing enmity between family members and different groups of people (4:1-24).

War (NRSV; NIV = *battle*) *within* (4:1) refers to the inner turmoil Christians experience as they try to decide between good and evil, between human desires (*earthly wisdom*, 3:15) and God's will (see Romans 7:7-24). The phrase does not refer to members of the church but to parts of the human body. If sin (war against God) dominates, then the human body is not a whole, not a unity, but one part fights against the other. (See Romans 6:13; 7:23; James 3:6.)

Kill (NIV; NRSV = *murder*) in James 4:2 probably does not refer literally to murder but to the kind of hostility between neighbors that has a desire (verse 4) to kill. Jesus said that even the desire to kill or hurt someone, a form of character assassination, is as good as murder. The intent in both cases is to destroy the other person (Matthew 5:21-26).

Coveting (verse 2), the desire to have what someone else has, has long been considered to be a serious spiritual problem in the world. The Bible warns that coveting is a serious offense, a violation of God's law (Exodus 20:17; Micah 2:2; Mark 4:18-19; 7:22; Romans 7:7; 13:9).

You ask and do not receive (verse 3) is similar to Jesus' sayings about the power of prayer (Matthew 7:8-10; 21:22; Luke 11:10-12; John 14:13). James has mentioned this principle before (see 1:5-6). See also 1 John 3:22; 5:14.

Adulterousness (verse 4) in the Scriptures refers frequently to women (or men) who are unfaithful to God, who break their vows to the Lord, who go chasing after other gods. See Psalm 50:18; Isaiah 57:3; Jeremiah 9:2; 23:10; Hosea 7:4; Matthew 12:39; 16:4. Perhaps this reference is an allusion to Proverbs 30:20, the way of an adulteress who feels no repentance for her evil activities.

One choosing *to be a friend of the world becomes an enemy to God* (verse 4). This is similar to the contrast Paul draws in Romans 12:2. Often in the New Testament the world is seen as a hostile place, waiting to lure the believer into sin and death (Luke 9:25; John 8:23; 12:19; 16:33; 17:14; 1 John 2:15; 4:5). One becomes an enemy of God through the rebellion of sin (Romans 5:10), and a dividing wall of hostility can exist between the nonbeliever and God (Ephesians 2:14-18). The only way to reconciliation is through Christ, who is our peace (Ephesians 2:14, 18; see James 3:18).

In verses 5-6 James indicates that he is citing two different quotations from Scripture to continue his discussion. The problem is that although verse 6 is clearly from Proverbs 3:34, the words in verse 5 cannot be identified with any text in the Old Testament. It is possible that James is merely alluding to a general Old Testament idea about God's jealousy, or that he is quoting a book that has been lost. In any case, both citations represent ideas that are very common in the Old Testament.

Jealously (NRSV; NIV = *envies intensely*, verse 5) does not refer to a petty or childish selfishness in God, but simply means that God is protective and will not tolerate persons who chase after other gods (verse 4, *adulteresses*) or ignore the gift they have been given (the *spirit which he has made to dwell in us*). For references to God's jealousy see Exodus 20:5; 34:14; Deuteronomy 4:24; 5:9: Joel 2:18; Nahum 1:2; 1 Corinthians 10:22.

The reference to God's willingness to support the humble but oppose the proud (verse 6) is picked up again in verse 10. Pride stands in opposition to repentance, and it is impossible for anyone to accept God's lead if he or she is dominated by total self-interest and rebellion against God (the essence of sin). In order to repent it is necessary to give up selfish pretensions and be humble before the God of all creation. Humility is a characteristic of Jesus (Matthew 21:5) and those who follow him (2 Corinthians 10:1; 12:21; 1 Peter 3:8; 5:5-6). It is a virtue repeatedly required in the Old Testament: Exodus 10:3; 2 Samuel 22:28; Job 22:23; Psalm 25:9; Proverbs 11:2; Isaiah 57:15.

A similar idea is repeated in verse 7 where James asks his readers to submit themselves to God and resist the devil. All people are to be humble before God and must submit themselves to God's will (Romans 8:7; 10:3; Hebrews 12:9). They will also be subject to Christ and be placed under his feet (Ephesians 1:22; Philippians 3:21; Hebrews 2:5-9; 1 Peter 3:22).

Although resistance and rebellion are signs of a sinful nature if used against God, they are virtues if they are used to oppose the tricks of Satan. The New Testament teaches that believers must always be ready to resist the devil. Refer to the discussions of James 3:6 and 3:15 above; see also Matthew 4:1-11; 13:39; Ephesians 4:27; 6:11, 2 Timothy 2:26; 1 Peter 5:8; Revelation 2:10; 20:10.

James indicates in verse 8 that the choice to submit to God and resist the devil must be resolute; there must be no waffling back and forth. His readers must not be of a *double mind*. As he has already said in 1:8, God will not give anything to those who cannot decide between good and evil. God will not tolerate those who say one thing and do another (2:1-7).

In verses 8-10 and the verses following, James shows how believers can live out the decision to follow God and God only. They can stay close to God, cleanse their hands, purify their hearts, mourn, and humble themselves.

Draw near refers to an attitude of worship and prayer before God, and is mentioned frequently in Hebrews as the key to finding forgiveness and grace (4:16; 7:19, 25). Cleansing the hands reminds readers of the Jewish practice of meticulously washing the hands before eating or handling holy objects (see Mark 7:1-8) and the belief that one must be ritually clean to draw near to God. In the Dead Sea community of Qumran believers even had to take cultic baths before they could worship properly. Purification was very important to all Jews and was accomplished through elaborate ceremonies of cleansing and sacrifice (see Leviticus 14:25; Numbers 31:23; Hebrews 9:22). James probably refers to activities of cleansing and purifying in a Christian sense, using them to indicate the necessity of keeping morally pure and free from sinful activity (*purify your hearts*; see also 2 Timothy 2:21; Titus 2:14; Hebrews 9:14; 1 John 3:3).

The order to mourn and weep in verse 9 is not a command to be sad or miserable; rather, it advises persons to repent for personal sins and the sins of the world. Possibly the command is taken from Jesus' teaching (Luke 6:21-25; see Isaiah 61:3; Amos 8:10). In order to draw near to God, Christians must be sorry for their sinful nature and must change their ways if they are to avoid judgment (see the warning to the rich in 5:1). They must also mourn when they see injustice in the world or oppression of the poor (2:1-7, 14-17; 5:1-6).

Who Are You to Judge Your Neighbor? (4:11-12)

In these verses James continues with the theme of humility and pride. Those who judge others are assuming God's role as Creator and Judge (Deuteronomy 32:35; Romans 12:19; Hebrews 10:30). They are also acting in a way that is contrary to Jesus' teaching that his followers should not judge others (Matthew 7:1-5; see Romans 2:1-8; 14:13-14). And they are ignoring that part of the Lord's Prayer which asks God to judge them as they judge their neighbors (Matthew 6:12-15). These verses also refer back to the concept of character assassination in 4:1-2 and warnings about the danger of evil speech in 3:9.

The Foolishness of Planning Ahead (4:13-17)

This section is loosely connected to 4:1-12 and the verses that follow in 5:1-6. It is a warning against the kind of pride and boasting that assume that as human beings we have complete control over our own lives. It is also a judgment on those who think that material goods are all they need for well-being (5:2-5). These verses are directed particularly against business people who, by the very nature of their work, have to plan ahead in order to manage their time and their inventory. What James says here is similar to the message of Jesus' parable of the rich fool whose planning could not keep him from the ultimate judgment of God (Luke 12:13-21).

Warnings against the illusion that life is not subject to chance or God's judgment run throughout the Bible (see Psalm 102:3; Job 7:7; Proverbs 27:1) and were common in Greek and Roman literature as well. James's prophetic words may be particularly important to modern Christians who live in a world where God and God's will rarely enter into daily life or planning. In our modern world, even Christians are so management-oriented that they hardly ever take God into account as they look ahead.

In verse 17 James capsulizes one of the main themes of his exhortation as he reminds his readers that faith without works is dead, that sin (rebellion against God), consists of knowing the right thing but refusing to do it.

§ § § § § § §

The Message of James 3:13–4:17

In this long section James loosely connects several important themes: the value of living according to God's wisdom (wisdom from above), the danger of hostility toward God and one's neighbors, and the value of humility as a way of drawing near to God.

In 4:7-17 he shows how that drawing near can be accomplished in practical terms: by spiritual purification (verse 8), by the avoidance of double standards and conflicting actions (verses 8, 17), by resisting evil (verse 7), by mourning for personal and corporate sins (verse 9), by avoiding character assassination of other people (verses 11-12), and by remembering that only God can control the future (verses 13-16).

§ § § § § § §

James 5:1-6

Introduction to These Verses

In 5:1-5 James intensifies a warning that has been
given earlier, namely that those who do not share their
wealth are in danger of God's judgment. See the
discussion above of 1:9-10; 2:1-7; 2:14-17; and 4:13-16.
Note particularly the summary of New Testament
perspectives of wealth and poverty in Part Four.

In chapter 5 it is not clear whether James is addressing
pagan plutocrats who are oppressing poor Christians
(verse 6), or writing to a church that has some members
in it who have considerable wealth, members whose love
of money (1 Timothy 6:10) has choked off their
compassion for others. The warning here is similar to the
ones given by Jesus (Matthew 6:19-21, 24-33; Luke 6:24;
12:13-21) and those found throughout the Old Testament
(Proverbs 11:7; 16:16; 28:6; Ecclesiastes 5:10-12; Amos
4:1-3; 5:10-13; 8:4-6).

Oppressors of the Poor, Beware (5:1-6)

Weep and wail recalls warnings of the Old Testament
prophets that God's judgment will be visited on those
who do not do God's will. See Isaiah 10:1-2; 13:6; 14:31;
15:2, 5; Ezekiel 21:12; Hosea 7:14; Amos 8:3. Misery is
another prophetic term that points to God's punishment
or to the age to come (Judges 10:16; Job 3:20-21; Romans
3:16; James 4:9).

In verses 2-3 the references to expensive goods and

jewels that will not survive no matter how valuable they are (*wealth, clothes, gold, silver*) are characteristic of warnings against the rich, a more poetic way of saying, "You cannot take it with you!" (See Matthew 6:19-20.)

The punishment that awaits the rich is that which God will bring at the end of time, in the *last days* (verse 3; John 6:39; Acts 2:17; 2 Timothy 3:1; Hebrews 1:2; 1 Peter 1:5; 2 Peter 3:3; Jude 18). It will bring about the separation of those who have done good from those who have done evil (John 5:25-28; Luke 16:19-31).

The words *eat your flesh like fire* also refer to judgment. (See Judith 16:17; also Numbers 12:12; Isaiah 30:27; Ezekiel 15:7; Amos 1:12, 14; 5:6; 7:4). *Flesh* stands for the person who will be punished and *fire* stands for the torment of Hell (see 3:6).

James gives specific examples of the exploitation of the poor in verses 4 and 6, which indicates that he is particularly concerned about the way the rich treat working people. In the ancient world, as in modern society, it was not unusual for laborers to be exploited, especially when there were no labor unions to protect them. Ancient literature is full of references to absentee landlords who did not pay workers well or take care of their needs. Jesus often referred to the tensions between owners and workers in his parables of the Kingdom (Mark 12:1-12; Luke 15; John 10:12). Workers who needed a daily wage to survive were constantly worried about being shortchanged (Leviticus 19:13; Deuteronomy 24:14-15; Jeremiah 22:13; Malachi 3:5; Matthew 20:8).

James uses another common image from the Old Testament when he writes in verse 4 that the wages of the laborers kept back by fraud *cry out* and the cries of the harvesters reach the Lord. The cries of the poor are heard by God because they are God's poor (Psalm 72:2), and they cause God to bring vengeance on those who oppress them (compare Genesis 4:10; Exodus 2:23; 1 Samuel 9:16; Psalm 72:12-14).

In verses 5-6 James indicates that the rich have continued to enjoy their wealth while the poor have undergone unimaginable horror. James's brief comment is reminiscent of the book of Amos, where the prophet castigates those who luxuriate in their riches while they grind the poor into the dirt. It also brings to mind Jesus' parable about the rich man who never sees the poor beggar who is at his door every day (Luke 16:19-31). The implication in James is similar to what Jesus said about those who are hypocrites, *they have received their reward* (Matthew 6:2).

Whether the rich have actually murdered the poor, as the language in verses 5 and 6 suggests, is not clear (*day of slaughter, murdered*; compare 4:1-2). Certainly, at the very least, those who are well off have contributed to the miserable quality of life of others who are economically deprived, a life that may be worse than death.

Scholars are not agreed about the meaning of verse 6, whether it refers to Jesus or to believers in general who do what is right in God's eyes. The phrase could also refer to the suffering servant of God, who did not lift up his voice in protest (Isaiah 42:1-3), or to Christ himself, who is called *the Righteous One* (or *the Just One*) in some New Testament passages (Acts 3:14; 7:52; 22:14; 1 Peter 3:18; 1 John 2:1, 29; 3:7). It is more likely, however, that James means the poor person who does God's will but still suffers at the hands of the rich.

In 5:16 *righteous man* (NIV; NRSV = *the righteous*) refers to any Christian who can use prayer to heal. However, in other passages it describes faithful believers in general (see, for example, Genesis 6:9; 18:24; Numbers 23:10; Ezekiel 3:21; Matthew 25:37, 46; Romans 5:7; 1 Peter 3:12). In James 5:6 surprise and dismay are expressed that people who are justified by their faith and works can still be put down by the rich and are too weak to offer any resistance. James's grief about the plight of the poor recalls passages found in the Old Testament that describe the suffering of the righteous, how their afflictions are many (Psalm 34:19), how the wicked plot against them (Psalm 37:12), how the righteous perish and no one cares (Isaiah 57:1), and how the wicked constantly surround them on all sides by the perversion of justice (Habakkuk 1:4).

§ § § § § § §

The Message of James 5:1-6

In this section James continues to express his concern for the poor, a major theme throughout his writing. Here he warns the rich directly that their wealth is perishable and will not protect them from God's judgment in the last days. They have been able to oppress the poor by holding back wages and living in luxury while others suffered. But the implication is that they will get what they deserve when God's judgment is finally revealed.

§ § § § § § §

James 5:7-11

Introduction to These Verses

James's advice about the need for patience is only loosely connected with the preceding verses. Probably he is thinking that even if poor Christians find themselves oppressed by the rich, they should not despair because they will get their reward when Jesus returns in triumph and judgment.

Be Patient, Jesus Is Coming (5:7-11)

Be patient is not a command to engage in wishful thinking. The Greek verb that James uses in verses 7 and 8 and the noun that appears in verse 10 (*patience*) both refer to gifts God gives to believers to get them through hard times. *Patience* (sometimes translated *forbearance*) is a mark of a servant of God (2 Corinthians 6:6). It is an attitude that enables Christians to inherit God's promises (Hebrews 6:12). It is a gift of the Holy Spirit (Galatians 5:22). See similar discussions in James 1:2-4, 12 where James writes about the steadfastness and endurance that God will give to those who trust God.

The event that Christians must patiently wait for, in spite of oppression and injustice, is the coming of the Lord (verse 7). *Coming* is the literal translation of the important New Testament word *parousia*. The Parousia was the event that was to bring history to a close, wrap up all of God's purposes in Christ, and bring final judgment.

When James says in verse 8 that *the coming of the Lord is near* he is expressing a desire and hope that Christians have had from the time of Jesus' death and resurrection—that Jesus would return again in power and judge the nations. James must have shared the view that Jesus might return at any moment, an opinion that appears to have been encouraged by Jesus himself (see Matthew 24–25; Mark 9:1). Paul and his followers were so certain of the immediacy of this great event that some members of the church sold their property and even gave up their jobs. Paul had to warn them in 1 Thessalonians 5 that even though he looked forward to the Parousia as much as they did, no one knew exactly when it would occur. Consequently, they should go about their daily lives, living as Christ would have them live.

James says in verse 8 that *the coming of the Lord is near.* Here he uses the same Greek word that Jesus uses in Mark 1:15 when he introduces his ministry. This same word is used similarly in Romans 13:12; Hebrews 10:25; 1 Peter 4:7. Clearly the coming of the Lord was not "at hand" if by that James meant that history would end at any moment. Thousands of years have passed and the Lord still has not come. Apparently the first Christians misunderstood Jesus' teachings and thought that he would return immediately when that was not what he meant at all.

As modern believers we can still yearn for a final consummation when Christ's power will be absolute in the world, when God will be *all in all* (NRSV; NIV = *everything in everyway* Ephesians 1:23; 3:19) and justice and peace will finally prevail. Until then, we must not be misled by those who predict the end of history every time there are rumors of wars, earthquakes, or other disasters. No one knows exactly when the Parousia will occur, whether in two minutes, in two days, or in two million years. In the meantime, we must trust in God's plan for us and for history, and be willing to serve God and do God's will, whatever it may be.

In the second half of verse 7 James uses the example of the farmer to illustrate what he means by patience. Since Palestine was largely a rural area, it is not surprising that biblical writers and Jesus often used pictures from farming to teach believers about God. James seems to be saying in verses 7-9 that Christians should be like the patient farmer. They may not understand everything that happens when the crops grow, but they can trust God and trust the process.

The words *door* or *doors* are used in the Bible to indicate God's judgment (Genesis 4:7; Luke 13:24, 25) and especially Jesus' power as judge (John 10:2, 9; Revelation 3:20; 4:1).

James concludes his call to patience with two examples in verses 10 and 11. *The prophets* refers either to the Old Testament prophets who witnessed to God in spite of opposition (see Luke 13:34; Romans 11:3; Hebrews 11) or to Christian prophets who were martyred because they preached the gospel.

§ § § § § § §

The Message of James 5:7-11

Advice is given here to the readers of James to be patient in spite of oppression and poverty. The Lord Jesus will come soon to judge all people, and then all persons will receive their deserved reward. As examples of patience James cites the common farmer (who trusts God's plan for growth even though he does not understand the science of growth), the steadfastness of the prophets, and Job, who held on to his belief in God no matter what happened.

§ § § § § § §

PART TEN James 5:12-20

Introduction to These Verses

This section may be divided into three main parts.
I. Take No Oaths (5:12)
II. Pray for Healing (5:13-18)
III. Correct the Backslider (5:19-20)

Take No Oaths (5:12)

James 5:12 is very similar to the warning in Matthew 5:33-37, where Jesus tells his disciples that they should not swear any oaths. Instead, they should be content only to say yes or no. Both pieces of advice were based on the fact that in the ancient world it was very common for people to take oaths on any number of things—gods, temples, the stars, the heavens above, the earth beneath—in order to swear that they were really telling the truth. Already in the Old Testament, even though oaths were often permitted, many passages warned that they must be taken very seriously (Jeremiah 5:2; 7:9; Hosea 4:2; Zechariah 5:3-4; Malachi 3:5). The Dead Sea Scrolls indicate that the Jews who lived at Qumran were forbidden to take oaths at all.

In this passage James is probably not thinking about oaths in a court of law, but about those that are used in everyday conversation. His idea seems to be that Christians must tell the truth at all times and always say what they mean. If everyone did that, there obviously would be no need for oaths. Since God brought the church forth by the *word of truth* (1:18), believers must never be false to *the truth* (3:14).

Pray for Healing (5:13-18)

In verses 13-18 James turns abruptly to give practical advice to those who are suffering hardship or illness. *Suffering* (NRSV; NIV = *in trouble*) refers to bad circumstances, literally *suffering bad things*. If anyone has distress, he or she should pray. In verse 14 James gives additional advice to those who are sick from an illness. They should call the elders of the church and let them do the praying.

In the second case, praying for the healing of the sick, a part of the life of the New Testament church is reflected that is unfamiliar to many modern Christians. Although some Christian groups still regularly participate in faith healing, most do not. The first Christians, however, were used to this practice, and the four Gospels are full of accounts of Jesus' healing miracles. These miracles indicate not only that the sick were healed, but also that faith was the main factor that brought forgiveness of sin and salvation as well (John 20:30-31).

James states in verses 15-16 that there is a direct connection not only between faith and healing but also between sin and healing. The Gospels indicate that Jesus healed many people and that he often attributed their cures to their strong faith in God and in him (Mark 2:5; 5:34). Others, however, were not healed, because of a lack of faith on their part or the part of people around them (see Matthew 17:20; Mark 6:5-6). Jesus also expected healing to be a part of the disciples' ministry, since they were called to *preach* the gospel, *cast out demons* (heal the sick), and *be with him* (Mark 3:14-15). The church carried out this healing ministry in his name (Acts 3; 1 Corinthians 12:28). Thus it is not difficult to understand why James thought that elders were capable of healing the sick.

The connection between healing and sin is much harder to appreciate. Today people often think that they are ill because they have done something wrong, and the Bible itself even makes a connection in some places between sin and suffering. Job's friends often warned him that his suffering must surely have been an indication that he had offended God in some way. (See also Luke 13:1-9.) When Jesus was asked, however, if such a connection existed, he completely rejected the idea that sin and illness were related. In John 9:3 he denies that people suffer physical illness because God is punishing them for sin.

In order to understand the tension between James's teaching in 5:1-18 and our own faith in modern medicine we need to remember that in the ancient world there was little knowledge of secondary causes. People could not imagine that wars were won or lost by human agency, that illness was caused by microscopic viruses, or that handicaps had genetic antecedents. Everything, for them, good or bad, was under the control of heavenly forces, God, the devil, or the gods.

We also need to realize that symptoms the first Christians usually attributed to demon possession are often better diagnosed today as genuine physical or mental illnesses. Mark 9:14-29 is a case in point, where the illness blamed on demon possession can be better understood in the modern world as epilepsy.

Elders in verse 14 is the translation of the Greek word *presbyteroi*, which literally refers to older men who had a reputation for wisdom. In the Christian church elders were appointed by the apostles to govern congregations (Acts 14:23; 15:2, 4; 20:17; 21:18; Titus 1:5). They had to be spiritually mature and morally correct in their behavior (1 Peter 5:1-5). James indicates that in the churches to which he wrote they still carried on the healing tradition given to the disciples and apostles.

Anointing . . . with oil in verse 14 refers to the belief, common in the ancient world, that olive oil had healing properties (see Isaiah 1:6; Mark 6:13; Luke 10:34). Oil is still used in some Christian traditions to anoint the sick and the dying. *In the name of the Lord* indicates the tendency of the first Christians to derive all their authority to heal and cast out demons from the power of Jesus (Mark 9:38; Luke 10:17; Acts 3:6, 16; 4:7, 10; 9:29). Verse 16 makes it clear that Christians regularly confessed their sins to one another and that some members of the church (perhaps the elders) had the authority to forgive sins (see Matthew 3:6; 16:19; 18:18; Acts 19:18; 1 John 1:9; 5:16).

James concludes this section, as he did 5:7-11, with an Old Testament example. In verses 17-18 he refers to Elijah as one who illustrates the power of a righteous person's prayer. Elijah's story is told for the most part in 1 Kings 17–18. In the New Testament he was considered to be one of the most important prophets, since Jews looked for him to appear before the messiah could come (Mark 6:15; 8:28; 9:13; Luke 1:17; John 1:21, 25). The information that Elijah prayed for three years and six months is not found in the Old Testament, but was common in later Jewish commentaries about his encounter with the priests of Baal (see also Luke 4:25).

Correct the Backslider (5:19-20)

Wanders from the truth indicates that James is dealing here with the problem of backsliders, those who have confessed faith in Jesus Christ but have denied that faith later or have not lived their lives in accordance with what they have said they believe. Thus at the end of his letter he returns to the place where he began, with his concern about believers who are double-minded (1:7). The concept of wandering from the right path is a common one in the Bible for describing the danger of idolatry or moral corruption (Ezekiel 33:10-11; Matthew 18:12-13; Mark 13:5-6; Ephesians 4:14; 1 Peter 2:25; 2 Peter 2:15).

It is not clear who the one is who will *be saved from death* in the last verse. It could be the backslider or the one who brings him back (verse 19). Some Christians believed that they were responsible for the correction of other believers who were sinning, and that if they did not do so properly, God might hold them accountable for the errors of their fellow members. Thus by "saving" someone else they might save themselves as well. Although such an interpretation is possible, it is more likely that James is speaking about the forgiveness of the sins of the backslider here and sees the church leaders in a healing role similar to that mentioned in 5:14-16.

For James's understanding of death see the discussions of 2:17 and 2:26 above.

Cover a multitude of sins refers to the idea that there is power to forgive sins and that all sins can be forgiven. Possibly James has Proverbs 10:12 in mind: *Hatred stirs up strife, but love covers all offenses* (NRSV).

James's homily ends rather abruptly on a note of love and pastoral concern, but without any reference to Jesus' role in forgiveness. Also there is no benediction or doxology like those that conclude every other New Testament letter.

§ § § § § § §

The Message of James 5:12-20

The final portion of James is completed with the author's pastoral concern for the weaker members of the church, those who have experienced setbacks, illness, or a loss of faith. James directs them to the power of prayer and indicates his belief that the leaders of the church must play a major role in the healing of the sick and the forgiveness of sins.

§ § § § § § §

Introduction to 1 Peter

Type and Style of Writing

Until recently Bible commentators were convinced that 1 Peter, like James and 1 John, was not a genuine letter, but was a tract or a baptismal sermon written for new converts. Now, however, most scholars think that it really is a genuine letter written to real congregations in four different parts of Asia Minor (modern Turkey).

First Peter has the essential elements of a real letter: the naming of the author (1:1), comments to the recipients and wishes for their spiritual health (1:2), inclusion of the name of the church member who delivers it (*Silvanus*, 5:12), a farewell from the author and others who are with him (5:13), and a peace benediction (5:14).

First Peter differs from personal letters in one respect. It is not sent to just one person or family, but it is written for congregations in four different areas. For this reason it is called a "circular letter" and was meant to be read and passed on to other Christians who were meeting in neighboring homes, cities, or provinces.

The letter, like other New Testament books, contains many different kinds of material. The author quotes or alludes to passages from the Old Testament in order to teach his readers about the Christian faith. The most obvious is 2:21-25, which is closely patterned after Isaiah 53, the chapter about the suffering servant. Numerous other passages are also quoted: Isaiah 40:6-9 in 1:24;

Isaiah 28:16 in 2:6; Psalm 118:22 in 2:7; Isaiah 8:14 in 2:8; and Psalm 34:12-16 in 3:10-12, to mention just a few.

In addition to the use of Scripture texts, the author of 1 Peter writes in a style that was popular in the first and second centuries called the "rhetorical style." The text is written in a highly polished, literate Greek, makes plays on words, has carefully constructed clauses, and utilizes compound negative words.

Other types of material are also used by the author. The letter is filled with advice given to servants and masters (2:18-20), husbands and wives (3:1-7), church leaders, called *elders* (5:1-4), and Christian believers in general (2:21-25; 3:8-12). First Peter also contains Christian hymns (1:20; 3:18-22), creeds, and prayers developed for new Christians (catechetical teachings).

Major Themes in 1 Peter

First Peter has four major themes that are found throughout the letter: (1) baptism and new birth, (2) encouragement in times of persecution, (3) the church as the true home of believers, and (4) advice for how to live successfully in an alien culture.

Authorship of 1 Peter

Although the first verse is attributed to the apostle Peter and the conclusion of the letter mentions the names of those who were associated with him (see 5:12-13), it is generally agreed that 1 Peter was written by a follower or admirer of Peter who was probably a member of a school or circle that was committed to Peter's teachings. Peter was known in church tradition for his connection with Rome (*Babylon* in 5:13 is a code word for the capital of the Roman Empire; see Revelation 14:8). It was there that Peter died.

The highly literate Greek of 1 Peter is not the kind of language a fisherman from Galilee would be expected to use, and some of the ideas in the letter come from periods that are relatively late in the development of the church. A number of passages show the influence of Paul's letter to the Romans, moreover, and indicate that 1 Peter was written at a time when its influence was well established, long after Peter and Paul had both died (about A.D. 64–65).

Recipients of the Letter

First Peter 1:1 indicates that the people who received the letter lived in five provinces of Asia Minor (what is now modern Turkey): *Pontus, Galatia, Cappadocia, Asia,* and *Bithynia.* The words *to the exiles of the Dispersion* (NRSV; NIV = *God's elect, scattered throughout)* do not necessarily mean that all of the readers were Jews. See the discussion of *dispersion* in the Introduction to James. More likely, the word is used as a sociological term to describe all the Christians in the area, Jews and Gentiles, who felt like refugees in a region where they were persecuted because their cultural upbringing and faith were different.

Date

Because 1 Peter mentions persecution and suffering at the hands of government officials, it is often assumed that the letter was written during one of the periods when the Romans made life difficult for Christians: the reigns of the emperors Nero (54–68), Domitian (81–96), or Trajan (98–117). It is also possible that the persecution mentioned was not official in nature but was of the type that happened from time to time when refugees and unfamiliar religions were introduced into new areas.

Because references to 1 Peter appear in 2 Peter (3:1) and in a writing called *The Martyrdom of Polycarp* (both written during the second century), 1 Peter was probably sent to Asia Minor sometime at the end of the first century during Domitian's reign.

1 Peter 1:1-2

Introduction to These Verses

The author of the letter identifies himself with *Peter, an apostle*. According to the Gospels Peter was the spokesperson for the disciples and had his name changed by Jesus from Simon (Matthew 16:16-19). He plays a leading role in the Gospel story (see Mark 8:29-30; 9:2; John 20:1-10; 21:15-23) and in Acts (2:14-42; 3:1-26; 9:32–11:19). Paul says in Galatians 2:8 that Peter was entrusted by God with the mission to the circumcised. According to tradition he was persecuted and died as a Christian martyr in Rome (John 21:18-19; 1 Peter 5:1).

Greetings (1:1-2)

The word *apostle* literally means *one who is sent out* and refers to a representative, an emissary, or a delegate. Such a person was often commissioned by a king or queen, for example, to represent the royal house in diplomatic negotiations. Although it is difficult to know precisely how people earned the right to use such a title in the early church, it appears that at the very least one had to have a direct commission from the risen Jesus and had to have certain gifts from the Holy Spirit to qualify (see Acts 1:1-26; 1 Corinthians 12:1-11, 29). Since all the Gospels report that Peter was one of the first to see the risen Lord, his authority as an apostle is not doubted.

For the meaning of *dispersion* see the Introduction to James.

The readers are addressed by the unusual title *exiles*.

Recent research indicates that the people who received this letter must have been living away from home as refugees or guest workers. Local residents apparently regarded them with suspicion and probably did not give them full legal and political rights. As Christians they were also alienated from their pagan neighbors because they had a different faith and code of ethics. See 1 Peter 2:11, where they are also called *aliens*. For similar expressions in the New Testament see Ephesians 2:19; Hebrews 11:13-16.

Pontus, Galatia, Cappadocia, Asia, and Bithynia were four Roman administrative districts in Asia Minor (Bithynia and Pontus made up one province). First Peter is a circular letter, and the author expected it to be passed around to the congregations in this large area. See Revelation 1–3, where messages are sent to seven cities.

Chosen and destined *by God* (verse 2) refers to the Christian concept of God's call to faith and ministry, that one becomes a follower of Christ not only through individual belief in Jesus but by the power of God's choice and foreknowledge. In the Old Testament special servants of God were given tasks by the direct summons of God. Examples are Abraham (Genesis 12:1-3), Moses, and the prophets (Isaiah 6:8, 9; Jeremiah 1:4-10). Paul indicated that God knows ahead of time what will happen and how people will respond (Romans 8:29-30; 9:11; see 1 Peter 1:20). He also believed that all Christians, not just apostles, are called to believe in Christ and serve God (Romans 1:6; 8:30; 1 Corinthians 1:26). For references to Jesus' call of the disciples see Mark 3:13-14; John 10:3.

For the meaning of *sprinkling with his blood* see the discussion of 1 John 1:7 below.

Verse 2 contains a reference to the Christian concept of the Trinity—how God can be Father, Spirit, and Son and still be one God. (See Matthew 28:19; 1 Corinthians 12:3-6; 2 Corinthians 13:14; Ephesians 4:4-6;

2 Thessalonians 2:13-14). Sanctification (*sanctified by the Spirit*) refers to the way in which God makes believers holy or sets them apart for a special ministry. (See 2 Thessalonians 2:13.) In 1 Peter, sanctification refers to baptism and being made new in Christ (1:23; 2:2).

The greetings end with a benediction wishing the readers *grace and peace* (see 2 Peter 1:2; Jude 2). *Grace* means something that brings happiness or good fortune, especially a gift or power given by God. In the New Testament grace is particularly connected to the mercy and forgiveness that comes through Jesus Christ (Galatians 2:20-21; 5:4).

As Paul points out in Romans, believers are made right with God not by keeping rules of the law, but by the gift of God in Christ (Romans 3:24; 4:16; 5:2). Although sin abounds in the world, the free gift of the grace of God abounds even more (Romans 5:15-17). The word *grace* is used frequently in 1 Peter (1:10, 13; 3:7; 4:10; 5:5, 10, 12).

Peace is also connected with forgiveness in Jesus Christ. For its meaning see the discussion of James 3:18 above.

§ § § § § § §

The Message of 1 Peter 1:1-2

The author of 1 Peter identifies himself with the apostle Peter, the disciple of Jesus. He writes to people who are political and spiritual refugees, those who are isolated from their neighbors because of their country of origin and their faith in Jesus Christ. He implies that they should not be discouraged since they have been called to their faith by God, made holy by the Spirit, and forgiven through the death of Jesus Christ.

§ § § § § § §

1 Peter 1:3–2:3

Introduction to These Verses

This section of 1 Peter has three main parts.
I. The Indestructible Faith in Christ (1:3-9)
II. The Witness of the Prophets (1:10-12)
III. Be Holy, as He Is Holy (1:13–2:3)

The Indestructible Faith in Christ (1:3-9)

This second section begins with a blessing of the
readers. In its most basic form *bless* means to *praise* or
glorify when it is given by human beings to God, and to
give benefits or to protect when it is something God does
for those who believe.

New birth (see 1:23; 2:2) may refer to the fact that many
of the readers are recent converts who have just
experienced the exhilaration of being transformed by
Christ. Christians know that believing in him makes
every aspect of life so different that it is not only *like*
being born over again, it *is* a whole new beginning (John
3:3, 5; Titus 3:5; 1 John 3:9). Paul uses a similar concept
when he writes about being a *new creation* (2 Corinthians
5:17; Galatians 6:15; compare Ephesians 2:10; Colossians
3:9-11).

Verses 6 and 7 refer to the fact that the readers of
1 Peter are undergoing difficult times as Christians. As
4:1-14 indicates, they are suffering for their faith and for
the fact that they call themselves by the name *Christian*.
Even though this time of testing is very painful, if they
look at their situation positively and think of it as the

kind of purifying that gold goes through, then they will realize that their suffering will give glory to God. For *trials* see James 1:2-15. Gold and silver are often used as symbols in the Old Testament (Psalm 66:10; Proverbs 17:3; Jeremiah 9:7; Malachi 3:3)

Without having *seen him* (verse 8) probably refers to the fact that even though the readers of 1 Peter are not eyewitnesses of Jesus' ministry or resurrection they can still love him and maintain their strong faith. In the New Testament those who believe without seeing are worthy of special honor (John 20:29; Romans 8:24-25; 2 Corinthians 5:7; Hebrews 11:27).

Souls in verse 9 refers not to the spirits or ghosts of people but to the whole person. The concept includes the physical and spiritual characteristics that make a person special. It is the essential person making up each individual that God wills to save. See John 12:27; Acts 2:43; 1 Thessalonians 5:23, 1 Peter 1:22; 2:25; 4:19; 2 Peter 2:8 where the same Greek word is used.

The Witness of the Prophets (1:10-12)

This section is directed very personally to the readers. The author wants to make sure that the individuals in the congregations take his message to heart.

The readers also need to understand that what they are hearing is nothing new. The essentials about Jesus Christ and faith in him have already been *prophesied*. Although it is possible that he refers here to particularly gifted Christian preachers who were called *prophets* (see the discussion of James 5:7-10 above), it is more likely that he means the writings of the Old Testament prophets. In several places he quotes them to show that Christ was already foreseen by them (1:24; 2:6-8; 3:10; 4:18).

Brought you good news (NRSV; NIV = *preached the gospel*, verse 12) comes from the Greek verb that has the same root as the word *gospel*. *Gospel* was not only a name applied to the first four books of the New Testament; it was also a term that summarized the basic message about Jesus Christ—his life, teachings, death, resurrection, and lifting up to the Father (Romans 1:1-6; 1 Corinthians 15:1-8).

Things into which angels long to look seems to indicate how privileged Christians are. Even though angels (the word comes from the same root as *gospel* and means *messengers*) are spiritual beings, they do not know as much about God's plan as believers in Christ do. Other New Testament passages also indicate that angels have limited powers (Mark 13:32; 1 Corinthians 2:9-10).

Be Holy, as He Is Holy (1:13–2:3)

In these verses the author offers strong words of encouragement to readers who are experiencing the pain of persecution.

Prepare your minds for action is in Greek *gird up your minds*, a biblical image (Job 38:3; Proverbs 31:17; Ephesians 6:14). Here it means, "Just as workers tuck their robes into their belts when they have hard work to do so nothing will get in their way, get your minds and hearts ready for the spiritual work ahead of you." *Be sober* also appears in 4:7 and 5:8. Although it can be a warning against excessive drinking, in this verse it probably urges Christians to remain in control and keep clear heads (1 Thessalonians 5:6, 8; 2 Timothy 4:5).

The standard of conduct that Christians should follow is provided by God. The words *you shall be holy, for I am holy* (verse 16) may come from Leviticus 11:44. *Holy* is an adjective from the same Greek root as the word *sanctified* in 1:2. As a noun it is often translated *saint*. To be holy means to be set apart for God, to be consecrated to God.

Believers are to give up desires that result in sinful behavior. Paul uses the same Greek word in Galatians 5:17, where he introduces a list of activities that are in conflict with the fruit of the Spirit. (See 1 Peter 2:16; 4:1-5.)

For *blood* (1:19) see 1:2. For *gold* see 1:7. The meaning of *exile* (NRSV; NIV = *live as strangers,* verse 17) is discussed in the Introduction.

Verses 20-21 provide the source of hope that Christians have: Their confidence and power come from God's plan from the beginning and the end. For a discussion of the Christian hope for the end of history see the comments on James 5:7-10 and 1 John 2:20-27. The author of 1 Peter is very concerned that readers understand and trust in the *coming* of Jesus when he will judge the world and wrap up history (see 1:5, 13; 2:12; 4:13; 5:1, 4).

Verses 22-24 explain how believers can be purified or made holy: They must obey the truth and have a sincere love for other Christians. The quotation in verse 24 is from Isaiah 40:6-9.

For *newborn babies* (verse 2) see the discussion of *new birth* in 1:3. Milk is a symbol of essential spiritual nourishment, which the word of God provides (see Isaiah 60:16; Hebrews 5:12-14). Possibly the author is implying that the readers should get the fundamentals of faith right before they try to master more complex theological truths. (See also 1 Corinthians 3:2.)

You have tasted the Lord is good is from Psalm 34:8.

§ § § § § § §

The Message of 1 Peter 1:3–2:3

This section lists the essentials of the Christian faith and provides encouragement to those who are persecuted. Even though believers are experiencing pain now, they can have confidence in the God who planned their salvation from the beginning, raised Jesus from the dead, and is preparing for the end of history.

§ § § § § § §

1 Peter 2:4–3:12

Introduction to These Chapters

This portion of 1 Peter may be divided into the following parts.

I. The Living Stone and the Living House (2:4-10)
II. Good Conduct Removes Alien Status (2:11–3:12)
   A. Set an example to the Gentiles (2:11-12)
   B. Relationships to government (2:13-17)
   C. House servants and masters (2:18-20)
   D. The example of Christ (2:21-25)
   E. Husbands and wives (3:1-7)
   F. Summary (3:8-12)

The Living Stone and the Living House (2:4-10)

Throughout this section several Scriptures are used to demonstrate that the church is built on Christ and that his coming was already foreseen by the Old Testament prophets. In verses 6-8 he uses Isaiah 28:16, Psalm 118:22 and Isaiah 8:14 to show how the symbol of the stone points to the coming of the messiah. In verses 9-10 he builds on Exodus 19:6, Isaiah 42:6-9; 43:20-21; 63:7-9 and Hosea 1:6, 9 to refer to the biblical idea of election, that is, the concept that God calls those who are to serve.

The expression *a stone* that will make men *stumble* (verse 8) refers to an obstacle that causes a person to trip and fall. Paul says that the cross and the salvation Jesus' death brings are stumbling blocks for the Jews. (See 1 Corinthians 1:23.)

The word *house* (verse 5) is used by the author to construct his idea that the church is the household of God. All the members are God's children (1:14) and live in a household where Christ is the head (2:7).

Set an Example to the Gentiles (2:11-12)

The verses that follow provide a *household code* for all those who want to be part of Christ's family. The author of 1 Peter uses the symbol of the house because the household was a basic unit in the society of the ancient world in Greece and Rome. Extended families (fathers, mothers, grandparents, children, and slaves) functioned as a unit and the members were bound together by strict codes of honor and duty.

In some circles it was believed that if order in the family could be preserved then all larger institutions could be expected to survive. If a father could not control his own house, on the other hand, how could he be expected to govern a city or a nation (or a church—see 1 Timothy 3:4-5)? The author of 1 Peter builds on this kind of understanding when he tells Christians that their household is constructed on a different order. The code is based, at its heart, on the example of Jesus Christ and his sacrificial love on the cross (2:21-25). Only he can finally rule a house, whether it is a private home or a church. See Romans 13:1; Ephesians 5:21–6:11; Colossians 3:18–4:1 for other Christian codes.

Relationship to Government (2:13-17)

The first example provides some political guidelines for Christians. The author seems to be anxious to urge his readers not to offend Roman officials. In such a way they will spare themselves further persecution, especially of an official nature. Since Christians had already endured terrible suffering under the maniacal emperor Nero (54–68), they had to be very careful. The basic idea is that believers should obey the normal rules of authority because these rules have been established to allow the peaceful running of society.

House Servants and Masters (2:18-20)

Here household slaves are told to endure their sufferings patiently, as Jesus suffered on the cross. The author clearly expects that many of his readers will be slave owners. In Philemon, even though Paul demonstrates a charitable attitude toward the way a slave should be treated, he supports the rule of secular law that slaves never have a right to emancipate themselves.

In 1 Peter Christian masters are not warned to follow Christ's example in their treatment of slaves as they are in Ephesians 6:9 and Colossians 4:1, but the same rule of love may be implied in 2:18 where the kind and gentle owners are mentioned.

The Example of Christ (2:21-25)

In this section all Christians are urged to be like slaves as they are admonished to follow the footsteps of Jesus, who suffered patiently for the sins of the world. The poetic interpretation in 1 Peter is based on Isaiah 52:13–53:12, the prophecy of the suffering servant. Christians believed that it was fulfilled in the death of Christ on the *tree* (NIV; NRSV = *cross*).

Jesus is not only the *lamb* (1:19) that is sacrificed for sin, but he is also the shepherd of the readers' souls. The shepherd was often used as a symbol for the caring activity of God or Jesus (Mark 6:34; 14:27; John 10:11-12) and was a title given to Christian pastors. The Greek word for *guardian* (NRSV; NIV = *Overseer*) here is the word from which we derive the words *episcopal* and *bishop*.

Husbands and Wives (3:1-7)

This section is similar to Ephesians 5:21-33 and Colossians 3:18-20, but it lacks the mutuality in those verses or the requirement to be subject to one another in the Lord Jesus Christ. Although the author of 1 Peter urges Christian husbands to treat their wives kindly as the joint heirs of the grace of life, the only reason he gives is so that their prayers will be answered more readily. In the Christian church today there is no room for a weaker or stronger sex. Husbands and wives and men and women must remain equal partners in Christ, fully accepted children before the same God.

For Sarah, a woman whom Christians often considered to be a model of faith, see Genesis 18:1-15; Galatians 4:21-30; Hebrews 11:11.

Summary (3:8-12)

The author sums up the rules of the Christian household by reminding all members to be united in their love for one another and to follow Jesus' example of non-retaliation. Verses 10-12 are an adaptation of Psalm 34:13-17. The key to Christian living, as he has said before, is to do right (2:12, 14, 20).

§ § § § § § §

The Message of 1 Peter 2:4–3:12

This section is constructed around several Old Testament texts and the symbolism of stones and houses. Although the readers are aliens and exiles, politically and spiritually, they can be assured that they are welcome in God's household. This house is built with Christ as the cornerstone and church members as the building blocks. Exhortation is given about the rules believers should follow in politics, master-slave relationships, marriage, and life in general. Above all they must follow Christ's example.

§ § § § § § §

1 Peter 3:13–4:19

Introduction to These Verses

This is one of the most difficult sections of 1 Peter. Those who desire a thorough understanding of these verses will need to consult a more detailed commentary.

Perspectives on Persecution (3:13–4:19)

Verses 13-17 continue a theme introduced earlier in the letter about the necessity of doing right (2:14-15, 20; 3:6, 11; see 3:17). The Christian's main goal, even in the face of persecution, should be good behavior (3:17). The Greek word for *behavior* means *way of life*, or *conduct*. It is used in 1 Peter in 1:15 and 2:12, and is also found in Ephesians 4:22 (*manner of life*). Practical examples of what the author means are given in 1:14, 22; 2:1, 11, 13–3:7; 4:9-10, 14-15. As he has already said in 2:18-25, if a believer is going to suffer, he or she should not do so as a common criminal, but as one being unjustly treated as a believer in Christ (3:17).

Be prepared to make a defense . . . to account for the hope that is in you (verse 15) helps those who may be mocked by their non-Christian neighbors or taken to court for their faith. They should use the situation to witness to their hope in Christ. (See Matthew 10:19-20.)

The next section, 3:18-22, is one of the most difficult in the New Testament, and it is impossible to know for certain what is meant here. The passage probably contains a Christian hymn that was used in worship services, but its meaning remains obscure.

The first part of verse 18 is clear enough. It is a classic statement of the meaning of Christ's death on the cross and the way his sacrifice delivers believers from sin. (See Romans 5:6; 1 Corinthians 15:3; Galatians 1:4; 1 Peter 2:24.) *Once for all* signifies that only one sacrifice, Christ's, is necessary for forgiveness of sins.

The second half of verse 18 through verse 20 (also see 4:6) is much more difficult. Who were the spirits Christ preached to, and where was the prison where they had to be visited? Scholars are generally agreed that because of the reference to Noah in verse 20 some of the spirits named here are certainly disobedient angels like those mentioned in Genesis 6:1-4. But it is also possible that the word *spirits* refers to human beings in general and the rebellion and sin that characterize human nature.

But where did these spirits dwell? The answer depends on the symbolism that influenced the author of 1 Peter. In Jewish tradition popular at the time this letter was written, the apocryphal book of 1 Enoch was very important. First Enoch is a symbolic writing similar in style to the book of Revelation. It describes the imprisonment of angels and the dreams Enoch (Genesis 5:21-24) had as he went through a series of heavens to announce judgment to the fallen spiritual powers. If this is the background of 1 Peter 3:18-20, then it would appear that the author is saying that after his ascension Jesus went into the heavens to deliver a message, either of judgment or of forgiveness, to the offending spirits. Thus in verse 22 it is said that Christ has gone into heaven and is at the right hand of God, with angels, authorities, and powers subject to him.

There is also another possible interpretation. Christian tradition records the idea that Jesus went on some kind of a downward journey after he died (Acts 2:27; Romans 10:7; Ephesians 4:9). Perhaps the author of 1 Peter is contending that Jesus descended into Hell and took the gospel message, probably to those who had died before he came into the world.

At the right hand of God (verse 22) is a reference to the early Christian belief that after Jesus' death, God raised him up to a place of special prominence and power in heaven. In the Bible, the hand is a symbol of power and authority (Exodus 13:3; 14:21; Deuteronomy 3:24; Job 19:21). God promises in Psalm 110:1 that only the messiah will have the ability to sit at the most important place of power, and that his enemies will be put at his feet. Christians believed that place to be given to Jesus (Mark 12:36; Acts 2:25; Hebrews 1:3).

Authorities and powers refer to spiritual beings that had control over humanity and certain areas of the heavens, and were often hostile to God (Romans 8:38-39; Galatians 4:3, 9; Ephesians 1:21; 6:12; Colossians 1:16).

In verse 21 the author states that all of Christ's preaching to the spirits corresponds to baptism. The connection he has in mind is this: Just as angels and human beings were disobedient to God in Noah's day, so they are now as the church suffers persecution at the hands of unbelievers. As Noah and his household (eight persons) remained faithful to God and were saved from the Flood, so faithful Christians in the *household* (NRSV; NIV = *family*) of God (4:17) are saved by water through baptism, being born anew and maintaining the faith they have in Christ.

In 4:1-11 the author returns to the importance of Christian ethical conduct. Christians are reminded again to retain their high standards of behavior and not to join in the immoral practices of the Gentiles. It is not easy in any age to follow the Ten Commandments and Christ's rule of loving God, neighbors, and even enemies (Matthew 5:43-48) when everyone else is acting very differently. Christians should look at it this way: Maybe by their good conduct they will persuade a nonbeliever to turn to Christ. The same advice was given earlier (3:1) to wives who had non-Christian husbands.

Verses 8-11 give some practical examples of proper behavior that are similar to the fruits and gifts of the Spirit mentioned elsewhere in the New Testament (Romans 12; 1 Corinthians 12; Ephesians 4). The section ends with a doxology (the Greek word for *glory* [NRSV; NIV = *praise*] is *doxa*).

Verses 12-19 contain a summary of what has been said before, and a final word of encouragement to believers. If they believe the words of the prophets (1:10-12), they will not be surprised at the painful purification they must endure (see 1:7). For the idea of rejoicing in times of trouble see James 1:2.

The readers of 1 Peter have suffered especially for bearing the name of Christ (verse 14). At first, *Christian* (verse 16) probably meant something like "little Christs," and was a term of derision (Acts 11:26; 26:28). But as more and more people suffered for their faith, they began to take it as a title of honor.

The section concludes with a citation of Proverbs 11:31. If it is hard to imagine how God forgives the sin of those who believe in Christ, what will happen to those who deliberately disobey God? Surely they will get what they deserve (verse 17). The readers of 1 Peter must hold fast and trust in the God who made them.

§ § § § § § §

The Message of 1 Peter 3:13–4:19

In this section the author urges his readers to continue with good behavior in spite of their suffering. Christ died for sins once and for all, and preached to the dead spirits, an action which reminds believers of baptism. By acting as Christians they may actually convert some of their accusers. All are reminded to be proud of the name *Christian* and to trust in God.

§ § § § § § §

1 Peter 5:1-11

Introduction to These Verses

In these verses the author summarizes several of the
themes that have appeared repeatedly throughout the
letter as he gives practical and spiritual advice to church
leaders (*elders*) and those who are either inexperienced in
the faith or recent converts (*younger*). The exhortation is
from a pastor to other pastors or church leaders. Those in
authority should work with the people of the church and
not use their power to dominate the congregation (see
Galatians 5:25–6:6). Those who are members must respect
the call of God and be subject to those who have
responsibility.

Advice to Church Leaders (5:1-11)

Verse 5 draws final attention to the household code,
which has been so important throughout the letter. Just
as believers must be subject or submissive to human
institutions, governors, and the emperor (2:13-17), slaves
must obey their masters (2:18), and wives must be
submissive to their husbands (3:1), so those who are
children in the church family must obey the leaders of
the congregation.

In verses 6-11 the readers are reminded of why they
need to be so humble. They are under the difficult stress
of persecution and they must depend upon God to help
them. (See Psalm 37:5; 55:22; Matthew 6:25-34; Hebrews
13:5-6.)

At the heart of their problem lies more than human

evil. They are also fighting the chief adversary, the devil (see the definitions in James 4:7; 1 John 3:8-9). He is called a *roaring lion* here because oppressors were often described this way in the Dead Sea Scrolls and other Jewish traditions (Psalm 22:13; Jeremiah 4:7; Ezekiel 19:6; 2 Timothy 4:17). The devil may have temporary power but it is God who calls the members of the church, not only to the present suffering, but to eternal glory. They are not to give in passively but are to actively resist evil (Ephesians 6:11-13; James 4:7). God will restore what was lost through suffering and sin, and will build them up and give them strength.

§ § § § § § §

The Message of 1 Peter 5:1-11

In the final chapter the author draws together several themes that have been important throughout the letter: God's call to eternal glory, the need to be subject to one another in the household of faith, and the support God will give believers who are suffering persecution. They must resist the devil who is behind all this trouble, and must trust in God's strength and love.

§ § § § § § §

1 **Peter 5:12-14**

Introduction to These Verses

In the final verses the author of 1 Peter reminds his readers why he has written: He is *encouraging* and *testifying* the truth about the grace of God. At such a perilous time, as he has stressed throughout the letter, proper Christian conduct is very important. So he turns their attention once more to his advice to *stand fast* in their faith. For the meaning of exhortation, see the Introduction to James.

Conclusions (5:12-14)

Silvanus is mentioned here affectionately as a *brother*, meaning that he was a coworker in Christ and a fellow Christian. The reference is probably to the church leader also named Silas in some texts who was Paul's frequent companion (2 Corinthians 1:19; 1 Thessalonians 1:1; 2 Thessalonians 1:1; Acts 15–17). He met Peter at the Jerusalem conference (see Acts 15:22-35).

Mark, or John Mark, was a relative (Colossians 4:10) of Barnabas (one of Paul's fellow missionaries). He was probably the same Mark whose family supported a house church (Acts 12:12) and who went as a young man with Paul, Silas, and Barnabas on the first missionary tour (Acts 12:25). When he left prematurely (Acts 13:5, 13), Paul was so angry with him that he would not let him rejoin his group. (See 2 Timothy 4:11; Philemon 24.) Later Christian tradition attributes the writing of the second Gospel to the same man.

My son is a pastoral term that an older Christian would use to address a pupil or younger colleague.

She (NIV) in verse 13 does not refer to the author's wife or a female member of his entourage, as is sometimes assumed. It is a symbolic reference to the congregation of which he is a part (NRSV; the Greek word for *church* is feminine). *Babylon* was the capital city of Babylonia, often mentioned in the Old Testament. Here it is a symbol for Rome, the capital of the Roman Empire.

The kiss of love describes the affectionate way Christians customarily greeted each other in the self-giving love of Christ (Romans 16:16; 1 Corinthians 16:20; 1 Thessalonians 5:26). The church used this greeting in later years as a regular part of the communion liturgy.

The letter ends with a blessing of peace for all that *are in Christ.* See the definition of peace in the discussion of James 3:18. Certainly this is an appropriate way to complete a letter written to people who must still endure the persecution of the church's enemies and the prowling attacks of the devil. The peace the author wishes for them is not just a temporary cessation of stress, but the eternal contentment and rest that can only come from believing in Jesus Christ.

§ § § § § § §

The Message of 1 Peter 5:12-14

The final words of 1 Peter mention two of the men who accompanied the apostle Peter and served as his coworkers. One last time believers are urged to conduct themselves as Christians and hold fast to their faith in God. *She who is in Babylon* is a symbolic way of sending greetings from the congregation in Rome. The letter ends with a blessing of peace for all those who are in Christ.

§ § § § § § §

Introduction to 2 Peter

Nature and Style of the Letter

Second Peter, although it claims to have been written
by the apostle Peter (1:1, 13-15, 17-19) shortly after the
completion of 1 Peter (3:1), clearly comes from a very
different environment from that which produced 1 Peter
(or the Gospels and Acts, in which Peter played an
important role). Along with Jude and Revelation, 2 Peter
is one of the latest and most unusual writings of the early
Christian church.

Second Peter is now an accepted part of the Bible, but
in the early church many Christians doubted its
scriptural value. The church leaders Eusebius (A.D.
263–340) and Jerome (A.D. 340–420) both denied that it
was Peter's work, and it was not accepted as an inspired
writing by the western church until the last part of the
fourth century. In form and style 2 Peter has common
features with later, non-biblical Christian writings often
called "pseudepigrapha" (false writings).

Similarities can be found between 2 Peter and
second-century Christian books that claimed to represent
Peter's thoughts or give the history of his life (*the
Apocalypse of Peter, the Acts of Peter, the Preaching of Peter,*
and *the Gospel of Peter*).

Like James and 1 John, 2 Peter is not a real letter but is
a sermon, a tract, or an encouraging homily. Its form is
very similar to Jewish writings called "testimonials," or

"valedictories." A testimonial was a farewell statement or "last will and testament" attributed to a famous person of faith that presented his final advice and predictions for the future (see 2 Peter 1:5-15; 3:3, 7, 10). Knowledgeable readers knew that the person represented in the testimonial had passed away long ago and that the author was really one of his disciples or someone who` wanted to gain authority for his own teaching by using a well-known figure's name. Books written after the Old Testament was completed often used this style of writing. Good examples are found in The Testament of Moses, The Testaments of the Twelve Patriarchs, The Testament of Job, and 1 Enoch.

Early Christians did not consider such a practice to be plagiarism but merely a way to spread the master's teaching. For the first believers, attaching Peter's name to 2 Peter pointed to the wonderful tradition that stood behind this new "letter" being circulated in the church.

Sources

Second Peter is made up of a rich tapestry of different sources. It refers to the Old Testament (1:20-21; 2:5-10; 2:22; 3:8), but does not quote it directly. Extensive use is made of the New Testament letter of Jude, incorporating almost the whole book (most of verses 4-18) in 2:1-18 and 3:1-3. Clearly, the author of 2 Peter had Jude in front of him. As a comparison of the two writings shows, he adapts parts of Jude to address the unique circumstances of the church or churches to which he writes.

The author also draws on Jewish traditions outside the Old Testament (2:4, 11-14) and his work has similarities to Christian letters and books written during the second century (such as 1 and 2 Clement and the *Shepherd of Hermas*).

Clear references are made to the Gospels (compare 2 Peter 1:14 to John 21:18; 2 Peter 1:16-18 to Mark 9:2-13 and other parallels; 2 Peter 2:20 to Matthew 12:45 and

Luke 11:26; 2 Peter 3:10 to Matthew 24:43 and Luke 12:39). In referring to the Gospels, the writer bolsters his connection to the apostle Peter.

Second Peter also makes an unusual statement about how difficult it is to understand Paul's writings (3:15-16), even though there is not much in the testimonial that resembles Paul's thought. Here Paul's letters have real authority, perhaps the authority of Scripture, and the author is worried about the way some Christians are misinterpreting them.

He also demonstrates that he is very familiar with pagan religions and philosophies that were popular in the Hellenistic world. Hellenism refers to the Greek culture that influenced most of the civilized world after it was conquered by Alexander the Great in the fourth century B.C. Second Peter uses several Greek words that are not found elsewhere in the Bible but are borrowed from the environment in which the author and his readers live. See the discussions below of *divine power* and *godliness* in 1:3-4, the virtues listed in 1:5-7, *putting aside* of my body (NIV; NRSV = *my death*) in 1:14, and *myths* (NRSV; NIV = *stories*) and *eyewitnesses* in 1:16.

The Situation

Because of the sources the author uses it is likely that he was writing to people who lived outside of Palestine and were influenced both by Jewish tradition and by pagan culture and religion. Verse 4 in chapter 1 indicates why he is writing the testimonial. He is worried that the Christian readers may lose their faith by being influenced by the corruption that is in the world. As 2:1-22 demonstrates, false teachers have come into the church, bringing destructive heresies and the denial of Jesus Christ as Lord (2:1, 20). They are also trying to get Christians to accept a system of conduct that is unchristian and unethical (1:5-8; 2:9-10, 18-22).

A second problem is equally important: 2 Peter's

readers are wondering whether Jesus will really come again as the prophets and apostles said he would (3:3-12). The testimonial is written to shore up their faith in and knowledge of Jesus Christ.

Although it is impossible to know for certain where the people who received 2 Peter lived, it is usually assumed that they were in Asia Minor (modern Turkey) or Egypt, places where Hellenistic culture and Judaism were both particularly strong. Because of the variety of temptations they faced (2:2-20), it is often suggested that they lived in a city environment, where any manner of evil could be found any time. Paul addresses similar concerns when he writes to the church in urban Corinth.

Authorship

The author of 2 Peter is an unknown church leader who uses Peter's name to add authority and prestige to the advice he is sending to some churches. It is impossible to know who the author was or where the letter was written. Because 2 Peter has little in common with 1 Peter, there is little evidence to suggest that the author belonged to the same school or circle that influenced the writing of 1 Peter (see the Introduction to 1 Peter, "Authorship").

Date of the Writing

Bible commentators have suggested possible dates of composition all the way from A.D. 60 (before Peter's death) to 160. Because of 2 Peter's adaptation of Jude, itself one of the last New Testament books, its use of pagan religious terms, and its similarities to Christian writings that were produced in the second century, it must be assigned a relatively late date, somewhere between 100 and 135. Commentators often suggest that 2 Peter was the last book in the New Testament to be written.

2 Peter 1

Introduction to This Chapter

Second Peter 1 may be outlined as follows.
I. Greetings (1:1-2)
II. Knowledge, Virtue, and Calling (1:3-11)
III. Peter's Own Experiences (1:12-21)

Greetings (1:1-2)

Second Peter begins with an opening salutation similar to those found in the other Catholic Epistles. The style and vocabulary indicate that the author is influenced by the Hellenistic culture in which he lives.

Peter is the name of Jesus' disciple used by the author to give his letter more authenticity. (See 1 Peter 1:1.) *Simeon* is Peter's Hebrew name (Matthew 4:18; 16:16-17; Mark 3:16; 14:37; John 1:40-41; Acts 11:13). Perhaps the name is added here so the letter will appear to have been written by an eyewitness to the events of Jesus' life.

A number of the words in the greeting are discussed in other parts of this commentary. For *apostle* see the comments on 1 Peter 1:1; for *grace* see 1 Peter 1:2; for *peace* see James 3:18; for *servant*, see James 1:1 and Jude 2.

In 2 Peter *faith* generally means a body of teaching or doctrine rather than an individual's belief in God's mercy. (See verse 5.) The author wants to assure his readers that their faith is not inferior to anyone else's, even if they are Gentiles and live in a pagan culture. (See also Acts 11:17.) The word *righteousness* serves the same purpose, and points to God's fairness and the equality given to all believers. (See 2:5, 21; 3:13.)

Knowledge is one of the author's favorite terms. It points to the truth about Jesus Christ that believers are given. Knowledge is the quality of faith that enables persons to resist the dishonest teaching of the false prophets. (See 1:3, 8; 2:20.)

Knowledge, Virtue, and Calling (1:3-10)

This section is written in the form of a farewell address given by Peter. (See the Introduction.) It employs the unusual expressions *godliness* and *participants in the divine nature* in verses 3, 4, and 7.

Godliness can be translated *piety, reverence,* or *religion.* The word is also found in 2 Peter 3:11. (See 1 Timothy 3:16; Titus 1:1) Godliness is based on affection with love (verse 7), and is the opposite of the uncaring and lying attitude of the ungodly (2:5-6; 3:7; see Jude 4, 15, 18).

Participants in the divine nature (verse 4) is a unique expression for a New Testament writer to use. Usually Christians speak about participating in Christ's suffering, not in God's nature. *Divine nature* was often used in Greek and Roman religions to indicate that humans, after death, would become immortal. Although the author of 2 Peter is thinking of the end of time and the coming of Jesus in power, it is possible that he has been so influenced by Hellenistic thought that he is suggesting here that the Christian soul will live forever in God. This idea is contrary, of course, to Paul's teaching in 1 Corinthians 15 about the resurrection of the body.

In verses 5-7 the author provides a list of virtues to help the readers in their ethical battle against the false prophets. *Goodness* means moral excellence or goodness. It was common in the ancient world for writers to provide lists to advise readers how to act properly. This list has many similarities to those found in Hellenistic religious and philosophical writings, which often began with knowledge and self-control. For other New Testament moral advice see Galatians 5:22-23; Ephesians 4:2-3, 32; Philippians 4:8; Colossians 3:12; 1 Timothy 4:12; 6:11; 2 Timothy 2:22; 1 Peter 3:8-9. The author has adapted the order of the list by ending it with the greatest Christian virtue and the best gift of God, love (see 1 Corinthians 13:13; Galatians 5:22).

In this passage the main idea is that God has given believers wonderful gifts and they must respond with appropriate behavior. The result will be that they will *never fall* (verse 10; see Jude 24), no matter what happens. They will receive the *eternal kingdom* (verse 11) as their reward.

As in the letter of 1 Peter, the concepts of the *call* and *election* (verses 3, 10) of God are very important here. Because God has chosen the readers to be believers and followers of Christ, they will be able to endure any temptation or hardship. (See the discussion of 1 Peter 1:2.)

The *promises* mentioned in verse 4 refer ahead to the certainty of the Lord's coming (1:16; 3:3-4) and the last day when all people will be judged. The false prophets deny these events; however, both happenings will surely take place even if it takes a long time (3:8-10).

The eternal kingdom (verse 11) refers to the same promise: Jesus will come again, the world will be judged, and there will be a new heaven and new earth (3:13). Then those who are godly will live with God forever. For the meaning of the similar expression *eternal life*, see the comments on 1 John 1:1-4.

Peter's Own Experiences (1:12-21)

In these verses the author continues with the testimony and reminiscences of the apostle Peter. The words *as long as I am in this body* (verse 13; see verse 14) indicate that the writer is still alive, but as the Introduction shows, Peter had died before 2 Peter was written. *Body* could literally be translated *tent*, and is a Hellenistic term for the human organism. (See 2 Corinthians 5:1-5.) Possibly the word is used in 2 Peter because of the association with Jesus' transfiguration (1:17-18) and the tents (*booths*) that are a part of the Gospel accounts. (See Mark 9:5.)

As our Lord Jesus Christ has made clear, verse 14, may be a reference to predictions made by Jesus about the type of death Peter would have (John 21:18-19).

The Greek word for *departure* in verse 15 is *exodus*, and may be used here to compare the Transfiguration and Jesus' coming to this other great event in Old Testament history when God saved the people from slavery and persecution.

In verses 16-21 the author uses the story of the Transfiguration (Matthew 17:1-8; Mark 9:2-23; Luke 9:28-36) to show that the prophecy (verses 19-21) about Jesus' coming is true. It is true because Peter himself was there as an eyewitness. For the meaning of *coming* (*parousia*) see the discussion of James 5:7.

For we did not follow cleverly devised myths (NRSV; NIV = *invented stories*, verse 16) is a response to the lies told by the false prophets who are upsetting the readers of 2 Peter. They must have said that the prediction of Jesus' coming again was a myth. Myths in the Hellenistic world referred to fantastic stories about gods and goddesses and human heroes. Sometimes people knew these myths were not literally true, but were only told to make a moral point. The author of 2 Peter assures his readers that the Transfiguration and the coming of Jesus are historical events, not pagan myths.

The word *eyewitnesses* in verse 16 is found only here in the New Testament and means *observer* or *spectator*. In some Greek mystery religions this word was used to describe those who were advanced members of the cult. Here it is used to relate the fact that Peter was a privileged member of Jesus' inner circle (see Mark 9:2; 14:33), one who was given the right to witness the Transfiguration firsthand.

In verse 19 reference is made to the *morning star* that *rises in your hearts.* In the ancient world divine beings and even kings were often called stars, and perhaps the author is demonstrating that Jesus' coming is greater than that of any other being, divine or human. (See the words of Jesus in Revelation 22:16; see also Numbers 24:17.)

Verses 20-21 are probably written to argue against further charges of the false prophets. No doubt they had said that the prophetic word in the Old Testament that pointed to the coming of the messiah was not really true and only a matter of interpretation and opinion. Clearly the author and his readers are struggling here with the difficult subject of how Scripture is inspired and how we can be sure that we understand it correctly. It is ironic, as the Introduction points out, that for many centuries Christians doubted that 2 Peter itself was inspired.

§ § § § § § §

The Message of 2 Peter 1

The first part of 2 Peter assures readers that the promises of God and the prophecies of the Old Testament are true. The Lord will come again, and those who have opposed him will be judged. Those who are faithful, however, will be given the eternal Kingdom.

Verses 12-21 are written in the form of a farewell address. The author uses the experiences of the apostle Peter at Jesus' transfiguration to show that the prophecies about him are not myths, but point to truth seen by Christian witnesses in actual historical events.

§ § § § § § §

2 Peter 2

Introduction to This Chapter

This part of 2 Peter concentrates an attack on the false prophets who are troubling the church. They are the ones who are truly giving their *own interpretation* (1:20), not the word of God.

The Danger of False Prophets (2:1-22)

Here, as in Jude 4, the licentiousness or moral perversity of the false prophets is seen as a major cause of their ungodliness. Compare verses 7, 10, 13, 14, 18, 20 for a list of their sexual indiscretions. They are also accused of being infected by greed (see verse 14). Their destruction (verse 3) and punishment (verse 9) are sure. The reference to the *destruction* which has not been asleep (verse 3) challenges the false prophets' charge that the day of judgment will never come, that God's condemnation is fast asleep. They will get their reward and all of their boasting will be in vain.

Second Peter 2 is based on Jude 4-16, and many of the key terms are examined in the discussion of Jude.

The words *cast* (NRSV; NIV = *sent*) *them into hell* (verse 4) are a translation of the Greek verb *tartaro*, which is used only here in the New Testament. In Hellenistic Greek mythology Tartarus was a place of punishment below Hell where the giant Titans were cast. Once again the author mixes biblical imagery with Hellenistic fable to make a point about his opponents.

Noah and the Flood are mentioned in verse 5 to provide a contrast between the righteousness of the godly and the disobedience of the angels who came down from heaven (Genesis 6:1-22). Here the Flood is a symbol of God's judgment on the ungodly. See the discussion of 1 Peter 3:20-21 and the connection made there between the ark and baptism.

Lot (verses 7-9) refers to the story of Abraham's nephew in Genesis 11–19. In particular, the author has in mind Genesis 18:23-33 and 19:1-29, where Abraham pleads with God to save the righteous people in Sodom and Gomorrah. The citizens of the cities were not spared, however, since not even ten people could be found who were not morally depraved. Some men of the city even wanted to make a sexual attack on angels carrying God's message. The reference to the *rescue* of the *godly* in verse 9 is probably to Lot and his family, who were saved, and also to all those in the church who remain faithful to God.

Verse 16 refers to the story of Balaam in Numbers 22:21-35.

Verses 18-21 may help explain the unusual statement in 3:15-16 that Paul's writings are hard to understand. Paul wrote many times about the concept of Christian freedom (1 Corinthians 8:8-9; 2 Corinthians 3:17; Galatians 2:4; 5:1, 13, 18). Probably the false prophets mentioned in 2 Peter 2:1 have perverted Paul's teaching into an enticement to immoral behavior. *They promise them freedom, but they themselves are slaves of corruption* (NRSV; NIV = *depravity*, verse 19) echoes Paul's teaching (Romans 6:16) and the words of Jesus (John 8:34) that if sin is confused with freedom, sin will always become the master. The false prophets have become libertines and are trying to corrupt other believers and lead them away from Christian virtue (1:5-9). Their freedom has led to even greater condemnation, because knowing the truth they willingly lived a lie. They would have been better off in ignorance (2:20-21).

The false teachers may also have been followers of the Epicurean philosophy, which maintained that the gods had no influence over humanity. Epicurus lived from around 342 to 270 B.C., and taught that superstition, fear, and uncontrolled passion ruined life. He urged his followers to avoid pain and seek true happiness. Nevertheless, the critics of the Epicureans often accused them of being interested in nothing but sensual pleasure. The bitter comments about the opponents' pleasure-seeking in verses 13-14 are probably an indirect attack on those who followed this way of life.

The chapter is summed up with threats against the opponents (2:22). *Wallowing in the mud* compares them to pigs, which were commonly used in Greek literature to symbolize the behavior of immoral people. Pigs may clean themselves, common wisdom claimed, only to return to the mud. *The dog returns to its own vomit* is from Proverbs 26:11, and indicates that the false prophets are so corrupt that they will keep returning to sexual perversity no matter how much they are warned. They are, to be sure, *irrational animals* (NRSV; NIV = *brute beasts*), *creatures of instinct* (2:12). For Jews, of course, dogs and pigs were particularly disgusting and to be compared to them was the ultimate insult (Deuteronomy 14:8; Mark 7:24-30).

§ § § § § § §

The Message of 2 Peter 2

Chapter 2 of 2 Peter is a condemnation of the false prophets who are spreading lies in the church and trying to lead the congregation into immoral behavior. Using examples taken from Jude, as well as the illustration of Lot, the author encourages those who are faithful to trust God to rescue them from trial.

§ § § § § § §

2 Peter 3

Introduction to This Chapter

The final chapter urges the readers to maintain their confidence in what they have been taught. No matter what scoffers say, the Lord will come again and the day of judgment will take place.

Is Christ Really Coming Again? (3:1-18)

Verse 1 refers back to the letter of 1 Peter, but it is unlikely that the same author wrote both books. See the Introduction to 2 Peter.

The reminder provided here is that believers should not forget the teaching of Jesus, delivered by the apostles, that immoral scoffers would come who would try to cast doubt on the coming and on the judgment of heaven and earth (verse 7). For possible meanings of *commandment* see the discussion of 1 John 2:7-14. Here the meaning includes the author's demand that his readers follow the virtues listed in chapter 1.

That the coming of the Lord would be accompanied by scoffers who would deny the truth of such an event or try to lead believers astray was a common one (see Mark 13:5-6; 1 Timothy 4:1-2; Jude 18). For the meaning of *coming* see the discussion of James 5:7-10. The words of the false teachers in verse 4 (all things have continued as they were *from the beginning of creation*) may be a criticism of Epicurean philosophy, which said that the gods did not influence the universe or human life.

The *day of judgment* (verse 7) refers to the end of the world when God will judge the ungodly. (See James 5:1-6.) Verses 8 and 9 indicate that this event may not take place in the readers' lifetime or even in the foreseeable future, but it will certainly happen. God has only one reason to delay punishment: the desire for more people to have an opportunity to repent and turn to Christ. The delay is parallel to the one in Sodom and Gomorrah (2:6-10). God wants to give all sinners time to reach repentance.

Verses 10 and 11 indicate that not just human sinners and rebellious angels will be destroyed at the end of time; the whole universe (*the elements*) will be dissolved with fire. Believers need not fear, however, because God will create new heavens and a new earth (see Isaiah 65:17; 66:22; Revelation 21:1). Thus, as Paul says in Romans 8:21-23, the whole creation is groaning for the coming of Christ and the gifts of the Holy Spirit.

The words *the day of the Lord will come like a thief* (verse 10) refer to the coming of the Lord. They echo the teaching of Jesus about the end of time (Matthew 24:43; Luke 12:39; 1 Thessalonians 5:2; Revelation 3:3; 16:15). Just as a thief does not announce plans to rob a house ahead of time, so no one knows when the day will be. So all must be ready at any moment for God's plan to unfold.

Since all these things prophesied by the Old Testament prophets and reinforced by Jesus will take place, the author of 2 Peter encourages his readers in verses 14-18 to be patient on the one hand, but excited on the other, about God's coming rule. Forbearance is a quality of Jesus that his followers also need.

For 2 Peter's comments on Paul (verses 15-16) see the Introduction and the discussion of 2:19-20.

Second Peter ends in verses 17-18 with final words of encouragement for believers not to be influenced by the *error of the lawless* and thereby lose their own stability. *Stability* (NRSV; NIV = *secure position*) is only found here in the New Testament, and means *firmness*. The verbal form *confirm, strengthen, establish* is used in Romans 16:25; 1 Thessalonians 3:2; 2 Thessalonians 3:3; Revelation 3:2. What is to be firmed up here is not just the readers' attitude but their faith in Jesus Christ and his coming. The same idea is put a little differently in James 5:8.

The last verse is a doxology much like the one in Jude 24-25. See the discussion there. The exhortation ends with the Jewish blessing *Amen* (*be it so*). Despite all the lies and distortions of the false prophets, the author of 2 Peter is absolutely confident that the coming of the Lord and the judgment will occur. *Amen* is a statement of that confidence and a final prayer, "Be sure to make it happen, O God!"

§ § § § § § §

The Message of 2 Peter 3

The last chapter of 2 Peter reminds believers of the predictions of the apostles and Jesus that the coming and judgment at the last day will surely take place. Not only will all beings on heaven and earth be judged, but a whole new universe will be created, all in God's own good time. Readers are to wait patiently for these events to take place and, in the meantime, give glory to God.

§ § § § § § §

Introduction to 1 John

Style and Main Themes

First John is one of the most beautiful, elegant, and moving books in the New Testament. Through the use of simple and straightforward language (the whole book has a vocabulary of only 303 Greek words) the author introduces readers to the fundamentals of the Christian faith. Indeed, Martin Luther said he had never read a book with such simple, yet expressive, words.

First John is not really a letter, but is more like a tract—a sermon or a guidebook for Christians. The author takes simple themes and shows them from two angles, from a positive and from a negative side, in order to make them easy to understand and give his readers an opportunity to choose between them. Throughout his tract he interweaves discussions about the beginning and the end of time (1:1; 2:17-18, 24; 3:8), life and death (1:1, 2; 2:18, 25; 3:14-15; 5:11-12, 13); light and darkness (1:5-10; 2:8-11); truth and falsehood (1:6-10; 2:4-5, 21-24, 26-27; 3:7, 18-19; 4:1, 6; 5:20), and love and hatred (1:5; 2:10-12, 15; 3:11-18; 4:7-21; 5:1-5).

Although John uses an uncomplicated style, it is not easy to determine the outline of his message. Because he does not move logically from one point to another but overlaps and interweaves the basic themes like the colors in an exquisite carpet, any outline a commentator provides has to be somewhat artificial. His thinking is not like a law brief that gives evidence in a tightly argued sequence; it is more like a spiral of ideas twisted and turned around each other into a braided strand of pearls. Because he makes it clear in 1:1-5, however, that his basic objective is to bring a fundamental message about Jesus Christ so that his readers might have fellowship with God and eternal life, the outline provided here concentrates on John's desire to bring that message, the major points of the message, and the dangers to the message.

The Situation of 1 John

Like many other books of the New Testament, 1 John was written because of problems created in the church by those who were opposed to the basic truth about Jesus Christ—rival preachers and teachers who tried to lead other believers astray. Scholars are not certain whether there was one group of opponents or more than one that troubled John and the Christians who were members of the church to which he wrote. John pits his own testimony against the message or messages they bring (1:2-3). In 2:18-19 he refers to them as *antichrists* who *went out from us, but they did not belong to us,* as if they were former members of his church who were trying to set up rival congregations. For this reason these opponents are often referred to as "secessionists," those who were dividing the Christian fellowship by trying to form new branches of it.

Although it is difficult to know what John's opponents taught, it is likely that they told people that Christians did not need to confess their sins to be forgiven (1:8-10; 2:1-2; 5:16-17) and that it was not necessary to accept Jesus as the Son of God to be close to God (2:22-25; 5:9-12). John's lengthy discussions of God's love and the necessity of extending that love to other people indicate that the opponents also failed to emphasize the need for Christian forgiveness and the importance of reaching out to the needy, as God had forgiven and reached out to the church in love through Christ. John knows that his opponents' view of the nature of Jesus Christ is completely wrong. In his tract he is determined to correct that view and show his readers who Jesus really is, teach them what it means to live as Christians, keep them out of the darkness of sin, and lead them to the light of truth and eternal life.

Authorship

The question of authorship in the three epistles of John is extremely complicated, and Bible scholars disagree about the true identity of John. From a superficial point of view, it is clear that 1, 2, and 3 John are closely connected to the Gospel of John. For that reason scholars have traditionally held that the apostle John, the disciple of Jesus, wrote all four books.

Many of the themes are identical, and it is obvious that the purposes in 1 John 1:1-5; 5:11-15 and John 20:30-31 and 21:24-25 are very similar. Early church tradition also attributed Revelation to the same man (Revelation 1:1, 4, 9; 22:8), and it was believed that John wrote all his books from the city of Ephesus.

As early as the third century, however, Origen wrote that some church leaders doubted that all the books were by the apostle. Although Eusebius (fourth century) believed the Gospel and 1 John to be authentic, he referred in his writings to the "so-called" Second and Third epistles of John, which, he said, might be the work of the evangelist or some other writer with the same name. Later, the man who translated the Bible into Latin, Jerome, said that the author of 1 John was not the same *elder* (see 2 John 1; 3 John 1) who wrote 2 and 3 John.

Although some scholars still think that 1, 2, and 3 John, the Gospel of John, and the Revelation to John were all written by the apostle, most modern commentators are agreed that it is not that easy to determine who the authors of all of these books were. The most likely solution is that 1, 2, and 3 John were all written over a period of time by the same author, and that this John closely patterned his letters after the Gospel, most of which was written by the apostle John. Clearly the epistles were written by someone who felt himself to be spiritually close to the author of the Gospel, and it is possible that he was even a student of his.

Most scholars recognize that the disciples who gathered around John the apostle at Ephesus formed a tightly-knit group that worked together to spread the truth about Jesus Christ by writing the last chapter of John's Gospel, the letters of John, and Revelation. It is possible that the epistles of John were written because disagreement arose in the school about the proper interpretation of the Gospel, and that the letters of John represent the "official" view of the majority of the members. The letters were thus written to refute the teaching of those who preached a different version and were trying to undermine the congregations established by the apostle and those who followed him. Throughout this commentary the author of the epistles will be referred to as John, even though more than one person may have been involved in writing the letters.

Place and Date

Because of the problems of determining who wrote the three letters, it is also difficult to know where the epistles were written and who received them. They were probably composed in Ephesus, the home base of the Johannine "school," and were sent to churches in Asia Minor (modern Turkey) that the apostle and his disciples founded. Since it is generally agreed that the Gospel of John could not have been written before A.D. 90–100, or even later, the epistles had to have been written sometime in the early part of the second century.

1 John 1:1-4

Introduction to These Verses

First John opens with a long, involved sentence that extends from verse 1 all the way through verse 3. In these verses and in verses 4-5 John declares his purpose for writing his tract: He wants to proclaim the message of truth about Jesus Christ to his readers and testify to it from his own experience.

Christ is from the Beginning (1:1-4)

The first verse of 1 John contains three key ideas: (1) the concept of the beginning; (2) John's understanding of the word of life; and (3) his testimony to what he has heard, seen, and touched.

(1) *Beginning* in verse 1 is the same Greek word that appears in the first sentence of the Gospel. *The word* probably reminded John's readers of Genesis 1:1 as well. Commentators disagree about the precise meaning of *beginning* in 1 John because they are not sure whether it refers to the beginning of Creation as it does in Genesis and John 1:1, the start of Jesus' ministry as the Son of God (his baptism, see Mark 1:1-11), or the church's first preaching about Jesus after the Resurrection (the beginning of proclamation).

Although all three events are important to John and are in his mind as he opens his epistle, his use of the word *beginning* in 1:1 most likely reflects the first alternative, namely that he is thinking of the lofty concept found in John 1:1-14, that Jesus participated with God in the creation of the world.

What John and those who believe as he does proclaim is not just a message *about* Jesus. The message *is* Jesus—his connection with God's eternal purposes and his eternal existence. This message is similar to the high concept of Christ found in Colossians 1:15-17.

(2) A second key to understanding 1 John 1 is the expression *the word of life*. Clearly, John has in mind the opening words of John 1:1. *The Word* (*logos* in Greek) is capitalized in the Gospel because it refers to Jesus Christ himself; it is not just a message about him. In the view of the author of the Gospel, God's word or promise became a living person in Jesus Christ (see John 1:14).

In the ancient world the concept of the *Logos* was important in philosophical and religious circles and referred, in various ways, to the principle or pattern that gave the universe its shape or meaning. Possibly John is in dialogue with some of these philosophies or is offering an alternative to them when he proclaims that the true *Logos* is really Jesus.

Even more important for John, however, is the idea found in the Old Testament that God's word is considered to be so powerful that it always does what it sets out to do (Genesis 1:1; Numbers 11:23; Deuteronomy 30:14; Psalm 119:89). The Word is eternal (Isaiah 40:8) and even takes on the characteristics of a living being (Proverbs 8:22-31; see Wisdom of Solomon 9:1-2).

In 1 John 1, John combines his understanding of Jesus as the eternal Word of God from the beginning with his desire to preach the word about him to his readers. As in other New Testament books, John may not have differentiated clearly between who Jesus was, is, and would become, and the message about him.

For many early Christians the word was many things at once: It was the Christian message about Jesus, it was Jesus' own preaching about the Kingdom, and it was

Jesus himself who was the Word from the beginning. (See Mark 1:15 and 4:1-20.) In 1 John 1:1 John is making a play on the word *logos* and is saying "The message we proclaimed to you from the beginning of our ministry when we brought you the proclamation found in John's Gospel is also God's Word from the beginning found in Jesus Christ the Son of God, who has been with us from eternity." The same word play is visible in 1 John 2:7, 13, 24-25 and 3:8.

Life in the expression *word of life* is another key term in John's Gospel, where it appears more than thirty times. The debate about the meaning of life is similar to those about *beginning* and *word*. Does it refer to the life-giving preaching that has been present since John and his colleagues began delivering it? Or does it have eternal dimensions? There are two possible solutions.

Life for John certainly involves the quality of living in this world, because he wants to protect his readers from the false message of his opponents. He wants them to avoid sin (1:8–2:6), do right (3:7), and put love into action (3:1-18; 4:7-21). Eternal life is a quality of living available to the believer here and now (see John 3:16; 4:14, 36; 5:24; 6:47; 17:2).

But John is also concerned about *eternal life* (1 John 1:2) and by that he means a life that has a starting point with God in eternity and ends there as well (2:24-25). By *eternal life* John means not only living but also the passage from death to life. This passage means love now for other Christians as well as freedom from the punishment of sin, which is both physical and spiritual death (3:14-15; see John 3:36; 8:51; 11:26). What God has given us as Christians, John argues, is eternal life. And eternal life is not only life connected with this world, but also life connected with God. God's life is shared with us exclusively through Jesus Christ. If you have Christ you have life; if he is absent in your life you are as good as dead already (5:12-13).

(3) The third key element that introduces John's readers to the purpose behind his message is found in verses 1-3, where he indicates that he and other Christians (*we*) have *heard, seen with our eyes, looked upon, touched with our hands,* and been shown (verse 2) that which was from the beginning, the message they now preach. At first glance, it might appear that John is saying that he is an eyewitness to the life of Jesus and that he heard Jesus' preaching, saw him perform miracles, and touched him during his lifetime and maybe even after his resurrection.

Although such a testimony would make sense if John were the apostle John who was Jesus' disciple, it is not credible, if, as most commentators agree, 1 John was written by someone who lived after the apostle had died (see the Introduction). Most scholars think, therefore, that John means one of two things by this testimony. Either John is testifying to the fact that he is one of the apostle's followers and heard his story, testimony that was based on an eyewitness account, or, as is more likely, he means that he belonged to a missionary circle that traced its origins back to the apostle.

If John believes he is bringing the truth about Jesus and knows it has been passed on by people who received it from Jesus' disciples, then he can say, in all honesty, that *we* (all of us who are in this group that follows the apostle) have seen, heard, and touched.

In verse 3 John indicates that he wants his readers to have fellowship with those who are in his circle and with God the Father. Because John's opponents are disrupting the church and teaching false doctrine, John is concerned that the love that Christians normally share with each other and with God will be disrupted. *Fellowship* is the common bond shared by people who believe in Jesus Christ (1 Corinthians 1:9). It is something believers experience through the power of the Holy Spirit (2 Corinthians 13:14).

Father (verses 2 and 3) appears with special frequency in John's Gospel, where it is found over 100 times and expresses the unique relationship between the Father and the Son (John 1:14, 18). In 1 John that same close relationship is repeatedly mentioned, a relationship that is also available to those who believe in Christ and are the children of God (1 John 2:1, 13-16; 3:1).

John completes the first section with a reference to the joy that will be complete if his readers live in fellowship with the Father. As the notes in the NIV and NRSV indicate, it is not clear whether John is referring to the joy he and his colleagues will feel (*our joy*) if the message is accepted, or to the joy of his readers (*your joy*). In 2 John 12 and 3 John 4 the author speaks about his own joy, and it is easy to see why he would be happy if the people in the church accept the truth. It is also possible to understand how his readers will gain immeasurable joy if they walk in the light and know Christ better.

§ § § § § § §

The Message of 1 John 1:1-4

In the first section of his tract John gives the reason why he is writing: He wants to proclaim the message about Jesus Christ, the Son of God, that he is the word of life. John builds on his readers' knowledge of the Gospel of John and calls them back to the lofty concepts of Jesus' identity introduced there.

The truth found in the Gospel is one which John and his colleagues testify to, and their testimony is based on the evidence presented by those who saw it with their own eyes. He wants the members of his church to accept this message because he wants to be sure that they have fellowship with God and with each other.

§ § § § § § §

1 John 1:5-10

Introduction to These Verses

John continues with his introduction of the Christian message he wants his readers to hear. *Message* in Greek is very similar to the word for *messenger* (*angelos*), which is translated *angel* in English. These words indicate that John and other believers in the church are preaching the Christian message or word about Jesus to his readers through their sermons and through the writing of the letter itself. In 1 John, John makes it clear that he is not giving just an opinion but rather a message directly from God or Jesus himself (*we have heard from him*). As he said in verses 1-4, it is God's own word.

God Is Light (1:5-10)

The heart of the message is that God is light rather than darkness. The contrast between light and darkness was commonly found in the philosophies and religions of the ancient world and in the Old Testament (see Psalm 139:12; Proverbs 4:18; Isaiah 5:20). This contrast was particularly prominent in the writings of the Jews who lived near the Dead Sea, and they used it to describe the battle with their religious enemies. One of their documents is appropriately called *The Scroll of the War Between the Sons of Light and the Sons of Darkness*. Perhaps John is thinking of their writings as he battles his own enemies who are also lost in darkness (compare especially 3:8, 10).

Perhaps John is also thinking of an ancient philosophy

called *Gnosticism*, which may have attracted some of his opponents in the church since Gnostic thought often made similar use of the light/dark symbolism. Gnosticism comes from the Greek word *gnosis* (*knowledge*), and refers to the belief that only Gnostics know who God really is. In some forms of Gnosticism it was believed that the God of the Old Testament who created the earth was a lesser god, a god of darkness rather than light, and that the role of religion was to bring the light of knowledge back to its original source. If some of John's opponents are saying that Jesus is the Son of an inferior god, he wants to assure his readers that their enemies are totally wrong. The God of Creation, the Father of Jesus, is nothing but light.

This same assurance is prominent in John's Gospel, (see especially John 1:4-9; 3:19-20; 8:12; 9:5). Throughout his epistles John continues to oppose the Gnostic idea that only they have the light and know God by encouraging his readers to be confident that they are the ones who really know God (1 John 2:3, 13-14), know the truth (2:21; 2 John 1), and know that they are of God (5:18-20).

When John tells his readers to *walk in the light* (verses 6-7), he may be thinking of Old Testament passages like Isaiah 2:5 or Psalm 119:105. *Walk* was a term used by both Jews and Gentiles to describe a religious or ethical way of life. Paul often employs the word to describe Christian living (Romans 8:4; 2 Corinthians 5:7). Walking is similar to the idea of "following" Jesus, which describes the Christian faith as an exciting pilgrimage behind the Lord of life (see Mark 1:18; 2:14, 15, for example).

In verses 6-10 John takes up the criticism of his opponents in some detail.

(1) Because they say they have no sin (verses 8 and 10) they have deceived themselves and are condemned to walk in the darkness. Although they claim to be in the

light, it is not true, and they can never have fellowship with God as long as they believe as they do.

(2) Because they deny that Jesus' sacrificial death on the cross cleanses them from sin (implied in verses 7 and 8), they have made God a liar and the word is not in them (verse 10). The key idea for John is *sin* and his opponents' contention that they are not sinners. The Old Testament claims that it is impossible to keep from sin (1 Kings 8:46; Proverbs 20:9), and Paul echoes the same belief in Romans 2:1, 3, 12 and especially in 3:9. In its most basic definition *sin* is opposition to God and revolt against God. In the New Testament it usually means "missing the mark" or "going in the wrong direction." Thus the expression *repent* from your sins in Mark 1:15 and other places literally means "change direction away from sinful activities."

Apparently John's opponents had developed some notion of Christian perfection (maybe as a misunderstanding of John's own teaching; see 3:6, 9). They believed that they no longer had to confess their sins or accept the necessity of Christ's death on the cross. John intends to stop such heretical thinking before it spreads and destroys the church. See further discussion of his concept of sin in the comments on 3:6, 8, 9 and 5:16, 18.

In John's view believers must accept the basic tenet of the Christian faith that no one can find forgiveness or draw near to God except through the cross. As he writes in verse 7, the blood of Jesus cleanses persons from all sin. By using the word *blood* John indicates that his understanding is a sacrificial one with Old Testament roots. Just as cattle and sheep had to be sacrificed in the Temple in order for the Jews to draw close to God (Exodus 24:8; Leviticus 17:11), Christians are put right with God by the blood of Christ shed on the cross. (See Ephesians 1:7; Colossians 1:20-22; Hebrews 10:19-22;

1 Peter 1:19; 1 John 5:6-8.) For the meaning of *purifies* (NIV; NRSV = *cleanses*) *us* see the discussion of James 4:8.

John continues to point to the absolute importance of forgiveness throughout his tract when he uses other words to describe the way God wipes away the consequences of sin (*forgive*, 1:9; 2:12; *take away*, 3:5; *destroy*, 3:8; and *atoning sacrifice*, 2:2; 4:10).

In verses 5-10 John argues that true Christians cannot say they have no sin. Instead they must confess (verses 8-9) their sin and ask for forgiveness. If they do not they will not have fellowship with God (1:3-4) or with each other (1:6-7). (See the discussion of 1 John 1:3 for a definition of *fellowship*.) They will also deceive themselves and make God out to be a liar (verse 10).

As the Introduction points out, the concept of truth and falsehood is very important for John. Here he presents it for the first time in verse 8. Clearly he is concerned that his readers may deceive themselves if they accept his opponents' arguments (see 2:26; 3:7; 2 John 7) and that they will not know the truth about Jesus Christ. Here again it is possible that he is arguing against some church members who may have accepted some form of Gnosticism, since *truth* was a key word for the Gnostics, too. Indeed, a later Gnostic writing was entitled *The Gospel of Truth*. For John there is only one way truth can be known, and that is through God and God's Son, Jesus Christ.

If John's opponents say they have not sinned, they deceive themselves and *the truth is not in* them (2:4). However, John goes further to say that if these opponents say they have no sin, then God is a liar (verse 10). For John it is inconceivable that God is a liar, because God is the very essence of truth (Hebrews 6:18). John knows that God's promises in the Scripture are true (Psalm 111:7; Isaiah 45:19; Titus 1:2), that Jesus' teaching about himself is true (John 14:6), and that his own teaching is true as well. "No," he argues, "it is not God who is the liar. It is you who have lied." "And," he implies, "you lie because you are connected with the *evil one* (see 2:13-14) who is *a liar and the father of lies*" (John 8:44).

At the end of this section John warns his readers that they must see the falsehood of the arguments of those who have separated themselves from the church. If they do not, they will suffer a terrible consequence, and it will be clear that the word of Jesus he mentions in 1:1-4 is not in them.

§ § § § § § §

The Message of 1 John 1:5-10

In these verses John defines the message he wishes to proclaim: God is light and in God there is no darkness at all. In this way he argues against his opponents who contend that God may be connected with darkness. In John's view God is light, and so is God's Son, Jesus Christ. Those who believe that they have not sinned and do not need the cross of Christ for the forgiveness of sins are the ones who are really in darkness. John's readers must take care, for if they accept such teaching the word of life will not be in them.

§ § § § § § §

1 John 2

Introduction to This Chapter

This chapter may be outlined as follows.
  I. The Danger of Sin (2:1-14)
      A. Do not sin (2:1-6)
      B. Walk in the light (2:7-14)
  II. The Danger of the World (2:15-17)
  III. The Danger of the Antichrist (2:18-29)

Do Not Sin (2:1-6)

John continues to express the anxiety already alluded to in 1:5-10 that church people under his care may be fooled into sinning and walking in the darkness. Here he indicates that he has a pastor's heart, one that reaches out with love and caring, when he calls his readers *my children* (verse 1). *Children* is an affectionate term that appears often in the New Testament pastoral tradition (1 Corinthians 4:14; Galatians 4:19; 1 Timothy 1:2; Philemon 10), and John uses it frequently as well.

As John indicates in verse 1, he hopes that the Christian children under his care will not sin, but in case they do he wants them to know that they have an advocate with the Father, Jesus Christ the righteous. *Advocate* (NRSV; NIV = *one who speaks in our defense*) is the English translation of the Greek word *paracletos*, which appears in Jesus' pastoral instruction to the disciples in John 14–16 in reference to the Holy Spirit. *Paracletos* means *one alongside to help*, and in the ancient world was used to describe someone who was a lawyer or counsel for the defense. The *advocate* was a person who stood up for a defendant before the judge and pleaded his or her case.

John wants his readers to know that Jesus not only died for them on the cross, but he will also be their attorney on judgment day. He will remind the Father that sinners are no longer his enemies but are now his beloved children. Jesus can do that because he has a close relationship with the Father (1:2-3) and because he himself is righteous; that is, he is just and innocent in all his ways and therefore has the standing to plead the case of others. (See the discussion of James 5:6.)

Although *atoning sacrifice for our sins* (verse 2) describes the way in which Jesus is able to bring a "not guilty" verdict for those who are sinners, scholars are uncertain precisely what John means here. This term is found only here and in 4:10, and is a difficult word to interpret. It comes from the Greek word referring to an action or activity that neutralizes or cancels sin. Uncertainty about John's meaning occurs here because the term is very similar to another biblical word, *propitiation*, which refers to something offered to God to turn away God's righteous wrath. *Atoning sacrifice* concentrates on the sin that causes a punishment to be called for, while *propitiation* focuses on God, who will do the punishing. The question then is, is John interested in the manner by which sin is forgiven or the reaction of God who does the forgiving? The most likely answer is that John has both ideas in mind. On the one hand, Jesus is the one who turns away God's anger at sin since he is the advocate who stands up for the sinner. On the other hand, he is also the means by which forgiveness is made possible because his act of dying on the cross cancels sin and makes the not-guilty verdict possible.

Not for ours only but also for the sins of the whole world refers to the fact that Jesus died for more than just the members of the church; he died for all people. *World* (*cosmos* in Greek) brings readers back to 1:1-4 and the cosmic assignment of Jesus Christ as first revealed in John's Gospel.

For discussions of the expressions *know him* (verse 3) and *liar* (verse 4) see 1:5-10.

For *perfected* (NRSV; NIV = *made complete*, verse 5) and abides *in him* (verse 6) see the discussion of 3:4-10.

Walk in the Light (2:7-14)

In this section John continues his pastoral concern by beginning with the word *beloved* (NRSV; NIV = *dear friends*), which comes from the Greek word *agape*. The word points to the self-giving sacrificial love of God, which is seen most clearly in Jesus Christ. (For a discussion of the New Testament concept of love, see James 2:8.) John uses the title *beloved* (see 3:2, 21; 4:1, 7, 11; 3 John 1, 2, 5, 11) to indicate that the readers are loved not only by John, as a pastor loves his flock, but also by God and by Christ.

In verses 7-14 John attempts to explain what he has already hinted at in 2:3-4, that in order to walk in the light and the truth believers must keep God's commandment of love, that is, they must heed the Old Testament law (see Leviticus 19:18) and Jesus' Golden Rule (see Matthew 22:39).

By the time John is writing, this commandment, along with the one to love God, had become the essential rule of Christian living (See Galatians 5:14; James 2:8). Thus John can say in verse 7, *I am writing you no new commandment.* This commandment motivated God to create the world in the first place; it is a well-known requirement of the Old Testament; and Christians have been taught it from the beginning of their spiritual lives.

Although John almost seems to reverse himself in the next verse when he says *yet I am writing you a new commandment,* he is not really doing so. There he means that in another sense the commandment of self-giving love as it is found in Jesus Christ is so amazing and runs so contrary to normal human experience that it almost seems like a new commandment sent straight from heaven.

In verses 9-11 John indicates that this love is to be realized most specifically by giving it to the Christian brother and sister. In a passage that is similar to James 2:1-17 and Galatians 5:13-15, John argues that anyone who hates his brother (or sister) cannot claim to be walking in the love of Christ. Since one of Jesus' primary teachings was that we should love our neighbors as ourselves, we cannot be in the light if our hearts are blinded by hatred. John will explain his thinking in more detail in relation to 3:10-18; see the discussion there.

In verses 12-14 John shifts gears somewhat and returns to pick up the thread of ideas he first introduced in 1:7-9 and 2:1-2 (the forgiveness of sins). Here he uses a clear pattern of stylistic repetition, which indicates that John's readers must have known the people or groups to whom he refers with these titles. However, we cannot determine for certain who they were. On a literal level they could be people of different ages who were in John's churches—infants, young people, and the elderly. Also, the words could be symbols that point to different levels of authority in the church, members who have just joined the congregation (*children*), church leaders (*fathers*), and those who had been in the church for a while (*young men* [NIV; NRSV = *people*]). Or, the titles may refer to different levels of spiritual maturity: new converts, those who have a certain amount of spiritual wisdom, and those who are the closest to Christ and are nearly perfected in faith (see 2:5; 3:9). A final option is that John is only speaking to two groups here rather than three, that *children* refers to all Christians whereas the other terms are for two groups often identified in early Christian churches: the church leaders, called *fathers*, and those who were recent converts (*young men*) and were still learning how to be faithful.

Evil one (verses 13 and 14; see 5:18-19) refers to Satan or the devil, who is the personification of evil. Apparently John is worried that the young men are particularly vulnerable to Satan's power, since he mentions the connection twice (verses 13 and 14) in relation to them. Evil is so prevalent that believers must decide whether to be children of God or children of the devil (3:10).

The Danger of the World (2:15-17)

In this passage John speaks of a different kind of love and a different world from the one he has referred to in previous verses. Although in 2:5 and 10 *love* means the self-giving love of God incarnated in Christ and given in fellowship to other Christians, in verse 15 it points to a perverted love that embraces things of this world contrary to the commandments of God. In verses 15-17, *world* does not mean the cosmos as it does in 1:1-4 or all of humanity as in 2:2. Rather, the word refers to the atmosphere of sin and corruption that pollutes and infects human life. John's usage is similar to what Paul refers to as the evil of the flesh (see Romans 7:18; 8:6; 1 Corinthians 3:1; 5:5; Galatians 5:17). John argues that it is not possible to love this world, since it is dominated by sin and characterized by passionate desire and greed. These things will all pass away when the hour of evil is over. In the meantime children of God should be content to do only God's will and not the will of the world (see Mark 3:35; Ephesians 5:15-17).

The Danger of the Antichrist (2:18-29)

In these verses John gives the final warning in this section. The *antichrist* (verses 18, 22) refers to the arch-enemy of God, the one who must finally be overcome by the Messiah, the Christ of God. In Greek the word *Christ* means *the anointed one,* and was a title given to priests or kings who were literally installed in office by having oil poured on their heads. Throughout the New Testament the word *Christ* refers to Jesus as the Messiah who will bring in the expected new age announced in the Old Testament (John 1:41; Acts 2:31-32; 3:18).

The word *antichrist* appears only here (verses 18, 22), in 4:3, and in 2 John 7. In the singular it refers to the evil one already mentioned in 2:13-14 (compare the *man of lawlessness* in 2 Thessalonians 2:1-12). In the plural (verse 22), John applies the word to his opponents in the church. He may use it here because some non-Christians, particularly Gnostics, may have anointed new members with oil as part of their initiation rites.

The last hour (verse 18) points to the belief of the early church that the final battle of faith was drawing near and that believers had to be prepared for the great conflagration at the end of time. For the use of *last hour* and the similar expression *last day* see John 6:39-40, 44, 54; James 5:3; 2 Peter 3:3. Christians believed that Christ would come at any moment to judge the world.

§ § § § § § §

The Message of 1 John 2

In this section John continues the discussion of the nature of sin begun in 1:5-10 and assures his fellow believers that their sins will be forgiven through the death of Jesus on the cross. Jesus himself will be their advocate when they stand before God as Judge.

In order to obtain forgiveness Christians need to live a life of love. If they truly want to walk in the light they must be sure to love one another. They must be certain that the temptations of the world, Satan (the Antichrist), and John's opponents (antichrists) do not destroy their faith.

§ § § § § § §

Introduction to These Chapters

This section may be divided into the following parts.
I. What It Means to Be God's Children (3:1-3)
II. Sin Is Not Compatible with Love (3:4-10)
III. Love One Another (3:11-24)
IV. Watch Out for False Prophets (4:1-6)
V. Love Comes from God Through Christ (4:7–5:5)
   A. Love comes from God (4:7-13)
   B. God's love abides in Christ (4:14–5:5)

What It Means to Be God's Children (3:1-3)

These verses are almost like a hymn. They ring with praise for God's love in Christ. John is so caught up in the amazing grace of God's love that he hardly knows how to express himself. The words *See what love* (NRSV; NIV = *How great is the love*) could literally be translated, *Consider how very much love the Father has given us.*

As was pointed out in reference to 2:1, *children* is an affectionate greeting that John reserves for the church community. Here, however, it means more, and points to the fact that Christians become God's children when they accept Jesus Christ, the unique Son of God. John's thinking is close to John 1:12-13, where it is said that people do not become children of God through physical birth or inheritance. They become God's children by believing in Jesus' name and being adopted as God's own sons and daughters.

In verse 1 *the world does not know us* probably refers to

the Gnostic notions of John's opponents. They mistakenly think they know all about God, but because they really do not know him or Jesus they do not understand those who are true believers (see 3:6). For the meaning of *world* see 2:15-17.

Verses 2 and 3 indicate that John is continuing to think about the coming of Jesus at the end of time (2:28). Those who believe in Jesus Christ are already God's children now. That is why John can address them with that title. But they are not everything that they will become. They still have to live in a world dominated by evil and they are still under the influence of sin (see 1:8; 2:2; 5:19). When he appears, however, everything will be changed. For then Christ will show himself in power and the whole world will be under his judgment. At that time the perfection of Christians in love (2:5) will be completed and those who believe in him will finally achieve their most ardent desire: They will be like him.

For similar passages that connect future hope with Christ's coming or glorification see Romans 8; 1 Corinthians 15:49, 51-57; 2 Corinthians 3:18; Philippians 3:21; Colossians 3:3-4; 2 Peter 1:3-4.

Sin Is Not Compatible with Love (3:4-10)

These verses present one of the most difficult sections of 1 John to understand, since they seem to contradict earlier passages. Although John clearly says in 2:1 that he knows that Christians sin, argues that those who say they do not sin are liars (1:8, 10), and discusses mortal sins in 5:16-17, in 3:6 and 3:9 he contends that believers who are in Christ do not commit sin at all. (See 5:18, 20.)

Over the centuries many different explanations of this discrepancy have been proposed, and a few of these explanations may be summarized as follows.

(1) Chapter 3 is written by a different writer from the writer of chapter 1 and thus the two sections appear to be

contradictory. Most modern scholars resist this solution because it is too simple an answer.

(2) When John says in 3:6 that those who abide in Jesus do not sin (present tense [NRSV]), he really means that they do not *keep on sinning* (NIV). Although Christians cannot help but sin, they do not do so as a habit or a constant practice. Their hope and aim is to eliminate the power of sin from their lives.

(3) John Wesley argued that whereas chapter 1 refers to spiritual infancy, chapter 3 discusses Christian maturity. The mature Christian will aim at the kind of perfection mentioned in Romans 6:1-4: Christians do not continue to sin but are planted together in the likeness of the death of Christ. Wesley drew a distinction between two types of sin. Although a Christian may be imperfect by mistake (through ignorance, illness, or temptation), real believers in Christ are free from deliberate sins.

(4) John is continuing the discussion begun in 3:1-2 and is drawing a distinction between the real and the ideal—between what is and what is to come. He knows that all human beings are sinners, but he also knows that perfection will come when Christ's reign is fully instituted. Christians have the seeds of the future in them and should start becoming what they already are: those who are forgiven and cleansed from sin.

Although solutions 2, 3, and 4 all have attractive points, the fourth possibility is the most consistent with what is known about the circumstances that forced John to write his epistles, and thus is the most acceptable. Apparently some of John's opponents argued either that they were free in this life from sin or that even if they did sin it did not matter. In their view, either way they did not need the forgiveness brought by Christ's death on the cross.

Against such ideas John argues in 1:8 and 10 that all people are sinners and must be cleansed from sin by the blood of Christ. In 3:6 and 9 he turns his attention from his enemies to the members of his church and changes his focus. Even though Christians are sinners and are living under lawlessness, they must not become discouraged. They can be confident that they are heading toward a new life in Jesus Christ. When Christ comes again (2:28), they will be entirely free from sin. In the meantime, they must start aiming for a life free from the power of sin. The goal is to be as much like Christ as possible, to be sinless as he was sinless (3:5), to be righteous as he was righteous (2:29), and to be God's children as he was God's unique Son. Those who abide in Christ know that they may have confidence on the day of judgment because love is perfected in them (2:5; 4:16-17).

Abides (NRSV; NIV = *lives*) *in him* (verse 6) contains a key word in John's thought that refers to the closeness believers can achieve with Christ. The word *abides* appears more than twenty-five times in 1 and 2 John and over thirty-five times in John's Gospel. The word expresses how Christians remain close to God (1 John 3:24; 4:13, 15), by abiding in the light (2:10), in the doctrine of Christ (2 John 9), in God's word (1 John 2:14, 24), and in the truth (2 John 2). Those who abide in Christ should walk in him (2:6) and know that they have eternal life (3:15).

Above all, John points out, his opponents do not abide with him or the members of his church because they do not have the love of God in them (2:1-6; 3:17).

In verses 8 and 10 John again draws a distinction between those who truly believe in God and those who are of the devil. (See the discussion of the evil one in 2:13-14.) *Sinning from the beginning* (verse 8) probably refers to the Jewish tradition that Satan was a fallen angel who existed with God from the beginning of the world. Christians do not have to worry, however, since the one who delivers them from the power of evil, Jesus Christ, has also existed from the beginning (1:1). In verse 10 the contrast between the children of God and the children of the devil is similar to references in the Dead Sea Scrolls where it is said that an angel of light and angel of darkness have existed from the beginning and that humanity is subsequently divided into two hostile camps, the sons of darkness and the sons of light. (See the discussion of light and darkness in Part 2.) What John says briefly in verse 10 will be expanded in 3:11–4:21: Children of God and children of the devil can be distinguished from one another by the way they extend God's love to others.

Love One Another (3:11-24)

John moves from the contrast between the children of God and the children of the devil to the centerpiece of his tract: the need for Christians to have love for their brothers and sisters. Since the epistle is not organized in a strictly sequential way (see the Introduction), this subject is not new here. John has already mentioned the fact that love for the Christian brother (or sister) is the absolute test of true faith in Christ (2:10, 11; 3:10).

In this section John reminds his readers that he is once again at the heart of his writing when he uses the expression *this is the message you have heard from the beginning* (see 1:5). He uses Cain as the primary example here because Cain was the first person, according to Genesis 4:1-24, to kill his brother (see Hebrews 11:4; Jude 11). For this sin he was driven out of the presence of God and retained a curse throughout his life.

John says that Cain was a son of the devil (*of the evil one*), thinking probably of Jesus' comment that Satan was a murderer from the beginning and the father of lies (John 8:44). John mentions Cain here for an obvious reason: The battle that the church is having with his opponents is a struggle among brothers and sisters. He hopes with all his heart that the struggle will stop and that God's will to love one another will be done.

But John wants to do more than speak about Cain's

connection with the devil. He also wants to speak about murder. Although there is no evidence to suggest that the struggle within John's church had actually come to blows, he says in verse 15 that *anyone who hates his brother is a murderer* (NIV). By this he means, no doubt, that hatred and the maligning of other Christians is a form of spiritual character assassination. (See Jesus' teaching in the Sermon on the Mount in Matthew 5:21-26.) What is more, by leading other Christians away from the truth in Jesus Christ, John's opponents are taking them down a path that leads to spiritual death and judgment (3:15).

In verses 16-18 John indicates that it is not only harmony in the church and spiritual life and death that are at stake here. Loving one another also has practical consequences. Here his argument is similar to James 2:14-26. Truly, faith that only talks about God's love, yet never gives that love away, kills rather than makes alive, and shows how true it is that faith without works is dead. For the early church's commitment to the poor (verse 17) see the discussion of James 2:14-26.

In verses 16 and 23-24 John returns to another of his reasons for writing his tract: He wants his readers to be sure to believe in Jesus Christ, the significance of his death on the cross, and the forgiveness they can receive in his name. Notice in verses 21-24 that John includes all three persons of the Trinity: God (verses 21, 22), the Son (verse 23), and the Holy Spirit (verse 24).

Watch Out for False Prophets (4:1-6)

Verse 1 begins with a play on the word *spirit* (*pneuma*), which was just used in 3:24 to refer to God's Holy Spirit. In contrast to the Spirit who is from God, John warns his readers to watch out for other spirits who are not. Just as there are two types of children, children of the devil and children of God (3:10), so there is a spirit of error and a spirit of truth (4:6).

Spirit in this section refers to human beings, namely

John's opponents, not angels or other heavenly beings. His warning is similar to that found elsewhere in the New Testament, where believers are told to watch out for false prophets who claim to speak by the power of the Holy Spirit (1 Corinthians 12:3; 2 Corinthians 11:4; 1 Timothy 4:1-4).

According to John, truth can be divided from falsehood by the way prophets speak about Jesus Christ (verses 2-3). Anyone who denies that Jesus has *come in the flesh* is not of God (see 2 John 7). Apparently some of John's opponents preached either that Jesus was not fully a human being (that he was a god in disguise who only seemed to be a man) or that he was really not fully God (only a human being). John denies both possibilities and pulls his readers back to John 1:1-14. In order to be a true Christian one has to believe that Jesus was God come in human flesh. (See Romans 10:9.) Debates like this raged in the church for centuries, and resulted later in the writing of the Nicene Creed and the Apostles' Creed to guide believers.

For the meaning of *antichrist* see the discussion of 2:18. For *world* see 2:15-17. *Listen* (verse 6) draws readers back to the vital importance of John's message (1:5; 3:1).

Love Comes from God (4:7-13)

John now discusses in detail the major point he has been driving at all along (see 2:10-11, 15; 3:10, 14, 17-18, 21, 23): The key to the Christian faith is love. In some ways, his thinking is parallel to Paul's in 1 Corinthians 13. Love is the greatest of all gifts from God and it leads to eternal life. It is the best of the fruits of the Holy Spirit (Galatians 5:22).

The section begins with the word *beloved* (NRSV; NIV = *dear friends*, see the discussion of 3:2), which indicates that those who truly believe in Jesus Christ already know what John is discussing. They are already wrapped in God's love and live in it every day. What kind of love do they experience? The love that comes directly from God and is the chief characteristic of God's nature (see 4:8, 16). "If you want to know what God is really like," John argues, "do not look for rules or definitions, doctrines or decrees. Just look for love." How do we know God loves us? Because God gave us a Son (John 3:16).

John wants his readers to understand how this great love came into the church. We do not get it by loving ourselves or other people first. Love can only be in us if it comes from its source, from God. As verse 10 implies, we cannot be taught how to love or even learn it from experience. It has to be a gift from God (see 4:19).

For *atoning sacrifice* see the comments on 2:2.

God's Love Abides in Christ (4:14–5:5)

This section repeats and expands several themes found earlier in the epistle: the necessity of confessing Jesus as the Son of God (2:23; 4:2-3), the fact that love can be perfected or matured in those who believe in Christ (2:5; 4:12, see 4:17-18), and the need for making sure that love is carried out in action (3:18).

Once again John involves all three persons in the Trinity in his discussion (see 3:21-24). Love comes from God because God is love. We see God's love because it is visible in Jesus Christ. We know that we abide in God because we have been given God's own Spirit (verse 13).

Savior (verse 14) means *one who rescues from danger*. It was a term occasionally applied to God in the Old Testament (Isaiah 43:3; Hosea 13:4) and is frequently used in the New Testament to describe Jesus' ability to bring about the forgiveness of sin (Luke 2:11; John 4:42; Philippians 3:20; 2 Peter 1:1, 11; 2:20).

In verses 20-21 John reminds his readers of the ultimate test that determines whether or not a person abides in God and believes in Christ: if he or she loves others (2:10-11; 3:10, 15-18). It is impossible to understand God's love only in a theoretical sense; it must be experienced in everyday living. It is impossible to love God, whose presence cannot be seen or touched, if we hate people who are around us every moment. If love comes from God it also flows the other way. Those who refuse to love and help others prove that love does not abide in them; they are not giving love to God's own children.

In 4:18 and 5:4-5 John gives the final word of hope to members of his church who are involved in a fierce struggle with opponents, antichrists, false prophets, and the spirit of error: If you have God's love in you, you do not have to fear or be anxious about spiritual defeat. The world, which so violently opposes the truth, will be overcome by Jesus Christ who gives us the victory (5:4). Those who believe in Jesus Christ as the Son of God will overcome the whole world (2:23; 4:2, 15).

§ § § § § § §

The Message of 1 John 3:1–5:5

These verses testify to the source of love that believers find in their hearts and experience in their lives: It comes from God. God is love by nature, and those who believe in God can give love to others because God has first given it to them. Anyone who claims to love God but hates other people is a liar, because it is impossible to know God's love without sharing it.

God's love is very powerful because it removes all fear. Opponents, antichrists, the devil, and false spirits are all impotent before God's love. Through Jesus Christ God has defeated all enemies and brings believers victory.

§ § § § § § §

Introduction to These Verses

In these verses John recapitulates several themes he
has mentioned before: *he who came* (2:28; 3:2), *testimony*
(1:2; 4:14), making God a *liar* (1:10), belief in Jesus Christ
as the *Son of God* (1:7; 5:5), *eternal life* (1:1-4), and *truth*
(1:6; 2:4; 3:18-19; 4:6).

Threefold Testimony (5:6-10)

Here John wants to finalize his argument about the
truth that is found in Jesus Christ the Son of God. In 1:2
and 1:5 he began his tract by witnessing to the truth of
the message he is bringing his readers. Chapter 5 talks
about witnessing to that message. In verses 6-10 he uses
words that come from the same Greek verb meaning *to
witness* nine different times in only seven verses. This is
the same root from which we derive our English word
martyr.

Whereas in 1:2 and 1:5 John refers to the testimony he
and those around him in his school can bring, here he
mentions three other witnesses as well: the water, the
blood, and the Spirit. He uses three witnesses because, in
a Jewish court of law and also for the group who wrote
the Dead Sea Scrolls, two witnesses were not always
enough to convince a judge of the truth. There had to be
three people who all said the same thing. "Thus," John is
saying, "the evidence is clear. Jesus really is proved to be
the Son of God."

What are the three witnesses? *Water* refers to Jesus'

121

baptism and the beginning of his ministry on earth, when God testified to the nature of the Son (see John 1:32-34). The *Spirit* is the Holy Spirit who is the best witness to the truth. According to John 1:32-34, the Spirit was present at Jesus' baptism. Possibly John may also be thinking of the fact that the Holy Spirit gives words to Christians when they are asked to testify to others (Romans 8:16, 26-27) and that he helps John and his colleagues testify against the secessionists. *Blood* points back to 1 John 1:7 and the cleansing action of Jesus' blood on the cross.

The three witnesses testify, therefore, to Jesus' whole life, his death, and the revelation of the truth in these events. They direct attention toward the forgiveness of sin and the way to eternal life. Through the Spirit the testimony leads outward from the Crucifixion to the present time, and the same Spirit, present at Jesus' baptism, testifies through John.

The final witness, and this is the fourth where only three are needed, is God (5:9-11). John has already shown that God is not a liar (1:10).

§ § § § § § §

The Message of 1 John 5:6-10

John concludes the argument he began in 1:1-4. His message brings the truth about Jesus Christ the Son of God, and only those who believe it can have eternal life. In addition to John's own witness, four other sources of testimony are available: the water, the blood of Christ, the Holy Spirit, and God. The evidence is unshakable: Truly, Jesus is the Son of God.

§ § § § § § §

1 John 5:11-21

Introduction to These Verses

This section has two major parts.
I. The Message Brings Eternal Life (5:11-13)
II. The Message Keeps Persons from Sin (5:14-21)

The Message Brings Eternal Life (5:11-13)

The testimony God brings is that believers have been given life through God's Son, Jesus Christ. Verses 12-13 repeat what has been said before: Only those who believe in Jesus Christ have eternal life (2:24-25; see also John 20:31). Thus 1 John ends as it began, with direct reference to the Gospel.

Name in verse 13 points to the belief in the ancient world that the name of a god or a divinity, just by itself, was a sign of power and majesty. Names indicated essence, definition, and nature. And Jesus' name, *Christ*, shows that he is the Messiah, the unique Son of God. Belief in Jesus' name is belief in his authority and power to forgive sins and in the God who sent him. It is through Jesus' name that all opponents and the devil will be defeated (see Mark 11:9; John 1:12; Acts 4:10; 1 Corinthians 1:2).

The Message Keeps Persons from Sin (5:14-21)

Verses 14-15 expand the reference in verse 13 to the power of Jesus' name. If Jesus' name is powerful, then it follows that prayers given in that name, according to God's will, certainly will be answered. John may be thinking of John 15:16 and 16:23-26, where Jesus promises his disciples that anything they ask for in God's name will be given.

The message of John concludes, however, not on this optimistic note, but with verses 16-17 that are very difficult to understand. Whereas in 3:6, 9 John made the puzzling assertion that there are some people who do not sin, here in verses 16-17 it is equally puzzling to read that there are others who are so terrible that they can never be forgiven.

Scholars look for possible parallels in Mark 3:29 where the unforgivable sin is mentioned, Mark 8:38 and Luke 12:9 where Jesus says that those who deny him will be denied before God, or Hebrews 6:4-9 where the writer states that those who turn away from the word of God cannot be restored to faith.

Mortal sin (NRSV) in verses 16 and 17 is a misleading translation of a Greek phrase that really means *leading toward death* (NIV). It certainly does not mean *deadly sin*, as it is often interpreted in the Roman Catholic tradition. John may not be thinking of different kinds of sin here, as if some sins were lightweight and others terribly significant. Perhaps he has in mind two different kinds of sinners: those whose beliefs and actions lead to light and eternal life, and those who live in darkness and deserve spiritual death and punishment.

John seems to end his letter on a rather tense and angry note. His opponents have caused the church so much trouble, and they are so immersed in darkness and committed to the devil, that there is no longer any point in praying for them. They, by leaving the church and betraying Christ, have put themselves beyond the reach of God because they are now children of the devil (3:10). As John says in 5:12, those who do not have the Son do not have life.

In verse 19 John leaves his readers with a message of

hope. They know that the Son has come and is in them. They abide in him and he abides in them.

The tract ends abruptly after John has repeated his main assertions about belief in the Son and the gift of eternal life. His warning, *Little children, keep yourselves from idols*, is totally unexpected. He has not mentioned idol worship before, and has not warned his readers anywhere about the foreign cults common throughout the ancient world that worshiped statues dedicated to various gods and goddesses. Although New Testament writers consider idol worship to be a dangerous temptation (Acts 17:29; Romans 1:23; 1 Corinthians 8:5-6), there is no preparation for this conclusion in 1 John. Perhaps it is merely an afterthought, or possibly John intends simply to finish with a general piece of advice: Do not submit yourselves to the idols you see all around you, and never give in to the substitutes for faith in God and in Jesus Christ that our opponents are trying to make you accept. Reject all false gods and all false ideas and live in Christ.

§ § § § § § §

The Message of 1 John 5:11-21

John's tract concludes with the confidence that believers may pray in Jesus' powerful name and expect their prayers to be answered. They are not to pray, however, for those who are so immersed in darkness that they are spiritually dead already. Believers can be confident that they will have eternal life even though the rest of the world is in the death-grip of the evil one. They must guard against all substitutes for faith in Jesus Christ as the Son of God, and must never worship idols.

§ § § § § § §

Introduction to 2 John

Unlike 1 John, where the author does not identify himself, the writer of 2 John immediately says who he is in the very first verse, where he calls himself *the elder*. In Greek the words *the elder* can be literally translated *the presbyter*. For centuries Christians have debated the meaning of this ambiguous title and have tried to determine who the presbyter was. The task is complicated by the fact that *presbyteros* can mean *old man, respected person,* or *a leader in the church* (see Acts 20:17; 1 Timothy 5:17; Titus 1:5; James 5:14; 1 Peter 5:1). Suggestions have been made that he was the apostle John in his old age; a man among a group of elders, who were each assigned different geographic areas in the church; a church leader named John who was not a disciple of Jesus and was not acquainted with the apostle John; or, as is most likely, a student of the apostle John who based his letters on the Gospel. In 2 and 3 John this John brings the apostle's message to the members of his church and refutes those who try to preach a different Christ. The title *elder* may indicate that the churches to which he is writing are under his administrative oversight and that he functions somewhat as a bishop.

Recipients

Second John also differs from 1 John because it appears to be written to specific persons, *the elect* (NRSV; NIV = *chosen*) *lady and her children* (verse 1), rather than to the church at large. Although most of the letters in the New

Testament are written to congregations, a few, like 1 and 2 Timothy, Titus, and Philemon, purport to be written to individuals.

Unfortunately, the identity of the recipient of the letter is not easily determined, since the Greek words for *elect lady* could have a number of different meanings. The word elect can mean *called of God* or *noble*, and was even used for a personal name in the ancient world. So suggestions have been made that *elect lady* should be translated *the lady Electa, the noble Kyria,* or *Dear Lady.* Such interpretations leave it unclear, however, who this lady is, why John refers to her children in verse 1, and why he ends the letter with the words *the children of your elect sister greet you* (verse 13).

Realizing that the word *children* could refer to members of a congregation rather than the sons or daughters of a particular person, most scholars now think that the words elect *lady* refer to a church rather than an individual. The word elect refers, therefore, to the call of the church members to be Christians. Verse 13 indicates that the letter comes from another congregation that contains other children of God. Perhaps John uses symbolic language because he does not want his opponents to know where these churches are if his letter should fall into the wrong hands.

Main Themes

2 John picks up several themes that are prominent in 1 John; truth (verse 2), love (verses 5-6), and the danger of deceivers and the Antichrist (verse 7). This letter appears to be a follow-up of 1 John, and was written at a time when the situation described there had deteriorated. Although some of the *children* (members) are following the truth, others are still being deceived.

2 John

Introduction to These Verses

Second John may be divided into four main parts.
I. Greetings (verses 1-3)
II. Follow the Love Commandment (verses 4-6)
III. Beware of Deceivers (verses 7-11)
IV. Conclusions (verses 12-13)

Greetings (verses 1-3)

Second John, unlike 1 John, is similar to personal
letters people routinely wrote in the first and second
centuries. It identifies the author and the recipients
(verse 1), gives greetings (verse 3), includes words of
thanksgiving about the readers (verse 4), and ends with a
farewell (verse 13). As the Introduction points out,
however, the letter is not to a single person but is to
members of one church from those in another.

For a discussion of *elect* (NRSV; NIV = *chosen*) *lady* and
her children see the Introduction. Many of the words used
in these verses have already appeared prominently in
1 John, such as *love, truth, know, abides,* and *Father*.

Whom I love in truth demonstrates that this letter is
written to an entire congregation. John is not in love with
one lady, but sends his love as a pastor to all the
members of the church. He hopes they will incorporate
the kind of love described in 1 John into their lives. *Know
the truth* (verse 1) refers not only to the fact that John
truly loves his readers, but also reminds them that they

must know the truth about Jesus if they really want to follow him.

Verse 3 expresses John's confidence that the truth will be victorious, since he gives his blessing in a future tense. *Grace* and *peace* are words often used in the introductions of New Testament letters. (See Romans 1:7; 1 Corinthians 1:1; Galatians 1:1; 1 Peter 1:1; 2 Peter 1:1.) *Mercy* is a characteristic of God and human beings. In the New Testament it usually refers to God's compassion and forgiving nature in Christ (Matthew 5:7; Luke 1:58; Romans 11:30-32; Ephesians 2:4). For *peace* see the discussion of James 3:17-18. For *grace* see 1 Peter 1:2.

Follow the Love Commandment (verses 4-6)

John expresses thanksgiving and joy (verse 4; verse 12) for his readers and for the fact that some of them do know the truth. See the discussion of *joy* in 1 John 1:4.

New command is probably a reference to 1 John 2:7-8. The new commandment is really an old one, and it is quite simple. As Christ commands them, they must love one another. The schism in the church has almost destroyed that love, and instead of love they are experiencing hatred and spiritual murder of one another (1 John 3:11-18). The commandment also has a second element. They must believe in the coming of Jesus Christ in the flesh.

For *beginning* see 1 John 1:1.

Beware of Deceivers (verses 7-11)

These verses indicate the deep concern John has for the churches that are his responsibility. The heresy his opponents have taught has been so widely accepted that the community is beginning to break up.

The *charge that they* will not acknowledge *Jesus Christ as coming in the flesh* shows that the deceivers are teaching gullible church members either that Jesus was not truly God in human flesh or that he only seemed to be a human being but was really God in disguise. (See 1 John 2:23; 4:2-3.) Either interpretation would be a degrading of Christ's mission, death, and resurrection, and is not the truth.

Many deceivers have gone out into the world (verse 7) means not only that John's opponents have defected from the truth his church teaches (1 John 2:19), but also that now they are pretending to be missionaries and are actively spreading their lies in other congregations.

Verse 8 warns about the dangers present at the end time when God's judgment is about to take place (see Mark 13:5, 9; Ephesians 5:15; Colossians 2:8).

Lose what you (NIV; NRSV = *we*) *have worked for* (verse 8) here and in the Gospel of John refers to members of the church and their faith, particularly a correct faith about the person of Jesus (see John 6:27, 39; 10:28; 17:12; 18:9). John is concerned not only that his church may lose members who defect to the deceivers, but also that his readers may lose the most important thing in the world, the truth about God. *Reward* is the result of faith that believers will realize at the end of time, if they will hold fast to their faith. At that time they will see God as God really is and will finally achieve their goal to be like Christ (1 John 3:2). For the idea of reward in the New Testament compare Matthew 5:12; Mark 9:41; 1 Corinthians 3:8-9.

The words *anyone who runs ahead* (NIV; NRSV = *goes beyond*, verse 9) describe John's opponents not only as those who have literally preceded him into church communities under his charge, but also as people who think they are better than others. (See the description of Diotrephes in 3 John 9.) *Goes ahead* may be a criticism of opponents who had accepted Gnostic ideas, since Gnostics often prided themselves on their superior and advanced knowledge. (See 1 John 1:1-5.)

Teaching of Christ (verse 9) refers to the teaching of John's community about Jesus, and more specifically about Jesus' teaching about himself and about the nature of love. John uses the word in 1 John 1:1-4 in the same two ways.

Do not receive him into the house (verse 10) is John's warning not to fraternize with deceivers in any way. Since they are liars and antichrists and are trying to lead others away from the truth about Jesus, they should be avoided by believers. *House* here does not refer to a person's dwelling but to churches, which often met in private homes (Romans 16:5; 1 Corinthians 16:19).

Conclusions (verses 12-13)

Paper and ink describes the way John sent his letter. He wrote it on a piece of papyrus, using an ink made of lampblack mixed in a gum thinned by water or vinegar.

I hope to come to (NRSV; NIV = *visit*) *you and talk with you face to face* may be a stock ending to a letter like "I miss you" or "see you later." In light of the serious problems in the church, however, it probably means that John is so upset about what is going on in the churches that he may have to make a personal trip to set things right.

§ § § § § § §

The Message of 2 John

Second John is a letter written by John and members of his church community to another church that is being misled by John's opponents. Thinking of the church as *she,* John warns the members not to accept a lie for the truth and lose their faith. John repeats several themes that were important ones in 1 John (love, truth, abiding in Christ, the commandment of love), and warns his readers not to have contact with deceivers.

§ § § § § § §

Introduction to 3 John

Third John, unlike 1 and 2 John, seems to be a personal letter rather than a message or warning to a congregation. Although the author is the same as 2 John (*the elder,* verse 1), the epistle is addressed directly to *beloved Gaius.*

This letter discusses some of the same subjects found in 1 and 2 John (*truth,* verses 3-4, 12; *love,* verse 6), but deals more specifically with three individuals. The letter brings encouragement to Gaius, chastizes Diotrephes for failing to acknowledge the elder's authority, and praises Demetrius because true believers have testified to the truth of his life and ministry.

Introduction to These Verses

Third John is the shortest book in the New Testament, consisting of only 219 Greek words. Although it has some of the key vocabulary from 1 and 2 John (*truth, beloved, testify*), 3 John is considerably different from its two predecessors. It is genuinely a letter since it is clearly written to an individual person rather than to a general audience or a congregation. Of all the so-called "letters" in the New Testament, moreover, 3 John has the closest resemblance to secular letters of the first and second centuries, even containing a wish for good health (verse 2).

The situation is also different from those presumed for 1 and 2 John. Two backgrounds are possible. Either 3 John is a totally independent writing that was sent to someone named Gaius to correct an isolated set of circumstances, or it continues to address the problems already addressed in the previous letters. Most commentators think the second possibility is the more likely. If so, deterioration of the situation described in 1 and 2 John must mean that more people are defecting to John's opponents and that he is getting more and more worried. The circumstances have become so critical that he has given up addressing his readers in general terms and is now being directly critical of one of the chief troublemakers, Diotrephes.

Third John may be divided into five main parts.

I. Greetings (verses 1-4)
II. Advice to Gaius (verses 5-8)
III. Criticism of Diotrephes (verses 9-10)
IV. Praise for Demetrius (verses 11-12)
V. Conclusions (verses 13-15)

Greetings (verses 1-4)

The elder (see the Introduction for the meaning of this title) begins his letter by addressing it to *beloved Gaius*. *Beloved* (NRSV; NIV = *Dear friend*) appears in verses 1, 2, 5, and 11. As the discussion of 1 John 3:2 demonstrates, this word is not only a term of affection. Its use indicates that John knows that Gaius believes the true message about Jesus Christ, that he loves Jesus and other church members, and that he is in the truth of Christ (*whom I love in the truth*). For *truth* (verses 1, 3, 4, 8, 12) see the Introduction and 1 John 1:5-10.

Who is Gaius? Gaius was a common name in the Roman world, and three different men appear in the New Testament with this name (one from Corinth, Romans 16:23; 1 Corinthians 1:14; another from Macedonia, Acts 19:29; and the third from Derbe, Acts 20:4). All these men were known to Paul. Although a fourth-century tradition identifies the Gaius of 3 John as a man who was later the bishop of Pergamum (a district of western Turkey), the evidence is inconclusive and it is not possible to know precisely who he was.

John indicates that Gaius is a man who can be trusted. He is someone who accepted the message of the gospel as John and his colleagues have preached it. The truth of Jesus Christ is evident in his life; he and others *walk in the truth* (verse 3); and he has loyally rendered *service to the brothers* (verse 5).

Commentators disagree about the nature of Gaius's relationship to the opponent Diotrephes, who is criticized in verses 9 and 10. Is Gaius a member or former member of a church headed by Diotrephes, and is he trying to correct the error of his pastor's ways? Or is he himself a pastor in a neighboring church who does not like what Diotrephes is doing? Whoever he is, he accepts John's authority and has gone out of his way to welcome those who have come from the mother church (verses 5-8) to correct the problems in Diotrephes' congregation.

The word *testified* (NRSV; NIV = *tell about*) in verse 3 is a translation of the same Greek verb meaning *testify* or *witness* that appears several times in 1 John (see the discussion of 1 John 5:6-11). John uses this word again in verses 3, 6 and 12.

Advice to Gaius (verses 5-8)

These verses, along with verse 3, provide important information about the situation behind 3 John. The author of the letter and members of his church circle were so worried about the situation in Gaius's locale that they sent leaders of the mother church to find out what was happening. These leaders reported Gaius's loyalty, but also told the elder that Diotrephes was dominating the church there and would not even talk to them (verse 10). Gaius's response was different, however, since he accepted John's authority (see verse 9) and helped finance their return visit.

Verses 5-7 provide some insight into missionary activities in the early church. Obviously John expects the churches under his care to provide hospitality to visiting preachers and church administrators. Hospitality was and still is a common characteristic of people who live in Greece and Turkey, and it was considered by Christians to be a gift of the Holy Spirit (see Romans 12:13; 1 Timothy 5:10; Hebrews 13:2; 1 Peter 4:9). Jesus said that anyone who welcomes those who are sent in his name welcomes him (Matthew 10:40; John 13:20). Paul and his associates were regularly assisted by local church people (Romans 16:1-4, 23; 1 Corinthians 16:6, 11).

Send them on their way (NIV, verse 6) and *they went out* (verse 7) are both technical expressions from the vocabulary of the early church to describe the support of the work of Christian messengers. Apparently the missionaries who came to Gaius's church accepted voluntary poverty (see Mark 6:7-12) and local congregations were expected to give them food and money.

Strangers describes fellow Christians who are strangers because they come from a distant area. They are brothers in Christ because they share the same Lord and the same faith, but they are still strangers to Gaius because he has never met them before.

The words *for the sake* in verse 7 are also misleading, because they should literally be translated *for his name*. *Name* describes the power behind the mighty name Jesus Christ (see the discussion of 1 John 5:13). It was in that name that Christian missionaries preached and healed.

Verse 8 is a technical missionary title given to those who were associates in preaching and teaching and who often traveled in the name of an apostle or elder and reported back to him. Paul uses the title many times to describe his friends and colleagues in Christ (Romans 16:3, 9, 21; 1 Corinthians 3:9; 2 Corinthians 8:23).

Criticism of Diotrephes (verses 9-10)

In verses 9-10 John turns to his main purpose for writing the letter: He wants to stop the influence of Diotrephes. Unfortunately, the letter is too short to determine precisely what this opponent of John actually did and who he was. John simply brings four charges against him. He does not acknowledge John's authority; he says bad things about John; he refuses to listen to those who represent the true church; and he is kicking out of the church members who support John and his understanding of the gospel.

Clearly Diotrephes had some power in the area in

which he and Gaius lived. Was he an elder as John was? Was he a pastor in one of the congregations? Was he merely a layman? Was he a bishop of that area who had betrayed his colleagues at church headquarters? Or worse yet, was he one of the antichrists or deceivers mentioned in 1 and 2 John? (See especially the discussion of 2 John 9.)

We cannot be certain about who Diotrephes was. What is certain is that he was leading church members away from the truth that John has testified to and written about. Because he did not think that John's teaching was correct, he would not recognize his authority as an elder or supervisor. And he would not allow himself to be interviewed by the church leaders who had come to visit the area. Finally, perhaps due to a misunderstanding of what John taught, Diotrephes was actually refusing church membership to those who supported John. He may even have been excommunicating them from the fellowship of the church.

Many commentators think the words *who likes to put himself first* (verse 9) indicate that 3 John points to a struggle for power in the church that eventually was to end in the establishment of the papacy in Rome. This letter clearly indicates that church leaders were beginning to battle over positions of authority. Who had the power to control the church where Gaius and Diotrephes lived? Should they take orders from John and follow his gospel tradition, or were they free to decide the doctrine and polity of their own congregation? Although such battles are inevitable considering the nature of human pride and sin, they certainly are a sad commentary on Christians' inability to unite in Christ.

Verse 9 indicates that John has written to Gaius's church before, and implies that no one but Diotrephes has seen it. It is unlikely that the letter referred to is 1 or 2 John, since those letters were obviously preserved for the church to be read by everyone. Probably Diotrephes destroyed the letter referred to in verse 9 and, as a result, it was lost forever.

Praise for Demetrius (verses 11-12)

If Diotrephes is someone for Gaius to avoid, John has just the opposite advice about Demetrius. Apparently Gaius does not know him, so John gives him an introduction and recommendation. Possibly he is the one who carries the letter. In the early church it was a common practice to provide testimonials for traveling missionaries (Acts 18:27; Romans 16:1-2).

Do not imitate evil but imitate good is similar to 1 John 2:6; 3:2; 4:17, where Christians are urged to be like Christ. Apparently Demetrius has demonstrated his trustworthiness as a messenger by doing good, a virtue held in high esteem in the church (1 Peter 2:12, 14-15). The way he lives his life shows that he is of God.

In verse 12 John wants to make sure that Gaius accepts Demetrius as an authentic envoy, so he uses the required three witnesses as he did in 1 John 5:6-12. In this case the witnesses are other people in the Christian community (compare verse 3), John's own recommendation, and the testimony of truth itself. By the latter John probably means that the truth about Jesus that finally is Jesus (John 8:32; 14:6; Ephesians 4:21) testifies about this Christian man because everything about him brings the message of God's love and truth. Demetrius clearly is one of those who *follow the truth* (verse 3).

Conclusions (verses 13-15)

The ending of the letter is similar to the conclusion to 2 John. See the discussion there.

The word *peace* in verse 13 is a common ending for a letter, especially in the Jewish tradition. Jews still use the Hebrew word *shalom* to say both hello and goodbye.

The letter concludes as John sends good wishes from other people in his congregation. *Greet the friends by name* is usually interpreted to mean simply "say hello to everyone." But it could mean that John knows many of the church members personally and he wants to make sure that Gaius gives them a special greeting, especially those who know the truth and support him and his ministry.

§ § § § § § §

The Message of 3 John

Third John is a personal letter from the elder to a church leader in one of the communities under his pastoral care. He has heard of Gaius's faithfulness from missionaries who have visited the church and he wants to give him some advice.

He encourages Gaius to continue to offer Christian hospitality to visiting preachers and teachers and to support them when they go on to other churches. He also warns him about Diotrephes, who is completely opposed to the elder's authority. Finally, he praises Demetrius for the manner of his life, which testifies to the truth about Jesus Christ.

§ § § § § § §

Introduction to Jude

Nature and Style

Jude, like 2 Peter, is sent to an unknown congregation or congregations and concerns the danger of false teachers. The author wants to keep his readers in the Christian fold, so he writes about *the salvation we share* and urges them to *contend for the faith* (verse 3). In verses 15-16 he gives several negative examples from Jewish tradition to show how bad the influence of his opponents is. What Christians are going through, he advises, is not surprising (verses 17-23). Those who understand the predictions of the apostles (verse 7) and are centered in the three-person God (verses 20-22) should expect such things. The letter ends with one of the most beautiful benedictions in the New Testament, in which believers are directed to the God and savior who will never let them fall (verses 24-25).

Jude has some similarities to other New Testament writings. Since it tries to preserve Jewish ethical values against pagan temptations, it is similar to James. Where it emphasizes the last days and the coming judgment of God, it is like 1 and 2 Peter and Revelation.

The style of the letter indicates that the author has been influenced by both Jewish and Greek thought. Many of his examples (Moses, Michael, Balaam) are from the Old Testament or later Jewish tradition. And his method of Scripture interpretation is similar to that used in the

Dead Sea Scrolls. The writer is also dependent on Jewish apocalyptic literature. Apocalyptic writings report mysterious revelations by God and his angels, and portray the divine will for the last days. Mark 13 (and parallels in Matthew and Luke) and Revelation provide other New Testament examples. In Jude reference is made to 1 Enoch and The Assumption of Moses (verses 6, 9, 12-16).

The author is also very familiar with Hellenistic Greek ideas (see the Introduction to 2 Peter) as his polished Greek style, his vocabulary, and his references to Greek religious and philosophical concepts clearly show. Jude must have been written to people in a culture that was strongly influenced by Jewish and Greek thought. The recipients probably lived either in Syria (where Jude may have been well-known), Asia Minor, or Egypt.

Situation

Although the whole letter is written to combat the ungodly persons mentioned in verse 4, it is never said who they really are. Scholars often argue that these persons might have been Gnostic heretics (see the definition of Gnosticism in the comments on 1 John 5:1-10). These heretics thought they had special knowledge (*gnosis*) and liberty from God.

Since the writer of Jude never discusses the meaning of the word *knowledge*, however, as the author of 1 John repeatedly does, and since he is not concerned about elemental spirits or matters of the *cosmos* (key ideas in Gnostic philosophy) as Ephesians (1:20-21; 3:10, 18) is, it is more likely that Jude's opponents are not Gnostic heretics but church members. Jude indicates that they are involved in church life and regularly take communion (*These are blemishes on your love feasts*, verse 12). Apparently the danger of their interpretation of the Christian faith is that they have misunderstood Jewish apocalyptic writings (verses 15-16) and are misleading the church about the nature of true Christian freedom. Perhaps they misconstrued Paul's teachings about Christian freedom and are urging members to become too libertine in their actions (see verses 4, 10, 11, 15, 16 in comparison with Romans 1:18-32; 3:8; 6:1, 15; Galatians 5:1, 13). Whoever the opponents are, Jude has only the harshest words for them (verses 10-13, 16).

Author

The author calls himself *Jude, a servant of Jesus Christ and brother of James* (verse 1). The implication is that he is the brother of the writer of the Book of James as well as the blood brother of Jesus (see Mark 6:3 and the Introduction to James). It is unlikely that such is the case, however, since the author of Jude does not identify himself with the apostles and sees them as respected men from the past (verse 17). Jude, however, would have known the apostles well, his brother James being one of them (Acts 12:17; 15:13; 1 Corinthians 15:7; Galatians 1:19, 2:9, 12). It is also unusual that Jude refers to himself as Jesus' *servant* rather than his *brother*. Jude, along with Jesus, furthermore, was raised in a Jewish Aramaic-speaking environment in Galilee, and would not be familiar with the Hellenistic-Greek ideas that are found in this book.

Although it is often suggested that the author could be another Jude, the one mentioned in Acts 1:13 (the son of James) or the Judas Barsabbas of Acts 15:22-34, it is best to conclude that the writer of Jude, like James, borrows the name of one of Jesus' brothers in order to increase the value and authority of his own writing. Who he really was remains a mystery.

Date

Because of the similarities of style and content, Jude was probably written around the same time as James, 1 Peter, and 1 John, at the end of the first century or the beginning of the second century.

Jude 1-4

Introduction to These Verses

Jude begins in the style of a letter, as all the other Catholic Epistles do. See the Introduction to 1 Peter.

Refuting the Ungodly (verses 1-4)

Most of the words in verses 1-2 have been defined elsewhere in the commentary. For *Jude* see the Introduction; for *servant* see James 1:1; for *James* see the Introduction to James and the Introduction to Jude; for *called* see 1 Peter 1:2; for *Father* see 1 John 1:1-4; for *peace* see James 3:18; 1 Peter 5:14; for *love* see James 2:1-3.

Mercy refers to a characteristic of God that is best recognized in the forgiveness that comes through the cross of Jesus Christ.

Kept for Jesus Christ (verse 1) is a reference to Jude's confidence that at the end of time, when God's judgment is exercised through the coming of Christ, believers will be kept safe by God and will receive salvation.

Beloved (NRSV; NIV = *Dear friends*, verses 1, 3, 17) is a title often used for Christians in the New Testament. (See Romans 12:19; 1 Peter 2:11; 1 John 2:7 for a few examples). Only those who are part of the self-giving love of God seen in Christ have a right to this title. People who are bonded in Christ have sincere love for one another.

Verses 3 and 4 give the reason why Jude has been written: The salvation of some of the saints is in jeopardy because of the sneaky tactics of the author's opponents.

143

Perhaps they were the kind of traveling preachers and teachers who troubled the churches to which John wrote.

Jude characterizes his opponents as ungodly persons (see verses 15, 18), that is, people who are so far from God in their beliefs and actions that they are irreverent or irreligious. Similar names are given unbelievers elsewhere in the New Testament (see Romans 1:18; 1 Timothy 1:9; 2 Peter 2:5, 6). Jude may have borrowed the word from 1 Enoch, where it is used several times.

In the writer's opinion ungodliness is particularly linked with sexual immorality (licentiousness). Acts 15:20 and the problems discussed in 1 Corinthians indicate that improper sexual behavior may have been an especially powerful temptation for Christians living in a pagan environment where some religions actually encouraged promiscuous activities.

When Jude writes that his readers must *contend for the faith* (verse 3) he means that they should actively fight sin, evil, and false teachings (see 1 Peter 5:9). In this verse *contend* is a term from athletic contests popular throughout the ancient world. Just as sports heroes often symbolize courage against great odds for young people today, in the first and second centuries the games were metaphors for the moral struggle against temptation. Similar images are used throughout the New Testament to encourage believers to train hard and fight for the faith (see Romans 15:30; 1 Corinthians 9:24-27; Philippians 4:3; 1 Timothy 6:12; 2 Timothy 4:7).

The word *faith* in verse 3 does not refer as much to individual beliefs as it does to the broader concept of the whole message about Jesus Christ, the gospel. In a sense, Jude is saying, "Be willing to fight it out for the basic proclamation of the good news about Jesus that some people are trying to undermine."

This faith, as he goes on to say, was *once for all entrusted to the saints. Entrusted* is a technical word used in the early church to describe the official way the

Christian message was passed on or transmitted from congregation to congregation. (Compare 1 Corinthians 11:2, 23.) Christians needed a sure way to distinguish true from false teaching.

We cannot be certain about the meaning of the claim that some who *long ago* were designated for *condemnation* (verse 4). The phrase may refer to the heavenly books in which the judgment of sinners was sealed. (See Revelation 20:12.) The phrase may also mean that the condemnation of the false teachers had already been prophesied by Christian writers (Acts 20:29-30; 1 Timothy 4:1-3; 2 Peter 2:1-3:7) or by the Old Testament prophets (Isaiah 9:15-16; Jeremiah 23:1-4). In any case, their fate is no secret: They will get what they deserve.

Jude concludes his initial indictment by saying that his opponents deny our only Master and Lord, Jesus Christ. The word *Master* (NRSV; NIV = *Sovereign*) is used only here in the New Testament. How they deny Christ is not entirely clear. Possibly they do so both by their loose sexual behavior (*licentiousness*) and by spreading falsehoods about the nature and identity of Jesus (see verse 24). Compare 1 John 2:22-23.

§ § § § § § §

The Message of Jude 1-4

The opening words of Jude bring a typical Christian greeting from the author and supply the reason why he is writing. Opponents are threatening the salvation of the readers, and Jude wants to encourage them to fight against falsehood. Those who have been misleading them have denied Jesus Christ by their words and actions, and they will get their just punishment.

§ § § § § § §

Jude 5-23

Introduction to These Verses

The second part of Jude is divided into two major sections. (1) Examples are given from the Old Testament and Jewish tradition of ungodly angels and irreverent people. Jude warns that behavior like theirs leads to condemnation (verses 5-16). (2) Advice is also provided not to be like them but to remain in the love of God (verses 17-23).

Do Not Be Like the Ungodly (verses 5-23)

In the first section the judgment of the ungodly is made clear. It leads to *condemnation* (verse 4), destruction (verse 5), loss of salvation (verse 5), and *eternal fire* (verse 7; see verse 23).

The initial example (verse 5) is taken from Numbers 14:1-35 and the story of Moses and the Israelites' exodus from Egypt. The Greek text of Jude is very difficult to interpret, and many ancient manuscripts have a variety of readings. In verse 5, for example, even though the NRSV and NIV read *Lord*, some Greek texts substitute the word *Jesus* for *Lord*. Although it may seem strange to modern readers to think of Jesus leading the slaves out of Egypt long before his birth, Christian interpreters often saw such connections. The Greek words for *Jesus* and *Joshua* are the same (meaning *one who saves*, Acts 7:45). Some early Christians may have believed that since Jesus was Lord from the beginning (see John 1:1-14), he was present at the Exodus and saved a people. (Compare 1 Corinthians 10:4.)

The point of verse 5 is that even though God saved the people from slavery there were some ungodly individuals among the Israelites who still did not believe in God, and they were later destroyed. (See Hebrews 3:7–4:11.)

The second example is taken from the apocryphal book of 1 Enoch, and is based on the story found in Genesis 6:1-4 where angels exceeded their heavenly boundaries and mated with human women. As the discussion in 1 Peter 3:19-20 shows, this story was very interesting to Christians as an illustration of the destructive power of sin (see also 2 Peter 2:4). First Enoch was a Jewish book written prior to the birth of Jesus, although parts of it were produced later and show Christian influence. In 1 Enoch 6–19 the story is told about the two hundred angels who came to earth with lust and ravaged human women. While they were there they taught humanity a number of other sins. The angels' children became giants in the earth and were responsible for all the evil that took place between the Flood and the final judgment day. Jude also makes use of 1 Enoch in several other passages.

Verse 7 draws attention to a similar example, the story of Sodom and Gomorrah and the surrounding cities (Genesis 19:24-29). The evil of these cities served as a model for God's judgment (Deuteronomy 29:23; Isaiah 1:9; 13:19; Matthew 10:15; 2 Peter 2:6). The story is compared to that of the angels in verses 5-6 to show how unnatural lust in heavenly or earthly beings, the kind of immoral sexual behavior Jude's ungodly opponents practice (verse 4), leads to God's punishment. Our modern word *sodomy* comes from Genesis 19:1-11, where it is told how men in Sodom wanted to rape angels sent with God's message. *Fire* is a reference to Hell. See the discussion of James 3:1-12.

In verse 9 the third example is given, that of the

archangel Michael. Michael is mentioned as the leading angel in Daniel 10:13; 12:1; Revelation 12:7; see 1 Thessalonians 4:16. The reference here is taken from a Jewish book written early in the first century called *The Assumption of Moses*. Although parts of the text have not been found, church leaders reported in later years that the book is about a contest between Michael and the devil for possession of Moses' body. Although the devil demands the body because he is the master of the earth, Michael will not surrender it to him. The point in Jude is that Michael does not argue with evil or condemn it but simply leaves judgment to God. The words *The Lord rebuke you* are from Zechariah 3:2.

Irrational animals (NRSV; NIV = *unreasoning animals*, verse 10) is similar to a reference found in the Apocrypha (Wisdom of Solomon 11:15), and means that the ungodly opponents are so infected by evil that they have lost all human reason and spirituality. They can only react by instinct, like wild brutes. The idea is elaborated in 2 Peter 2:10-13. Compare Galatians 5:15.

Verses 11 and 12 provide additional examples of those who opposed God, Cain and Balaam. In Jewish tradition Cain was considered to be a murderer, and was thought to be in league with the devil. See the discussion of 1 John 3:11-24 (especially verse 12). The story of Balaam is told in Numbers 22–24 and 31:8, 16. In the Old Testament there appear to be two different assessments of Balaam. Nehemiah 13:2 condemns him for his curse, whereas Micah 6:5 indicates that his answer to the king served God. Jude favors the former and uses Balaam as an example of someone who would take a bribe and do anything for money (see also 2 Peter 2:14). Revelation 2:14 warns against the teachings of Balaam, which encouraged the Israelites to eat food sacrificed to idols and to practice immorality. Jude may have this tradition in mind too, since his ungodly opponents are licentious (verse 4).

Korah's rebellion (verse 11) refers to Numbers 16:1-35 and the story of the opposition of Korah and two other men to Moses' leadership. In this context the story points either to the opposition of Jude's opponents to his ministry or to the rebellion of the ungodly against the law given by God to Moses. This verse begins with a prophetic announcement of the woe that is to come, as in James 5:1. See the discussion there.

Verses 12 and 13 are allusions to 1 Enoch 2–5 and chapter 80. In 80:2-8 Enoch refers to punishment of the ungodly and uses many of the same negative names for them as are found here in Jude. The faults of the ungodly influence other believers and their presence at the love feasts is ruining worship and fellowship. *Love feasts* (after the Greek word *agape*) means the Lord's Supper, a sacrament that was based on the self-giving love of Jesus Christ on the cross. The meaning of agape love and the way in which communion services were disrupted by the unfaithful have been discussed in reference to James 2:1-3. (See also 2 Peter 2:13.)

In verse 12, as the footnote in the NRSV demonstrates, the third word may be translated *reefs* rather than *blemishes*. If blemishes is the correct reading, the meaning is that the ungodly cannot make the pure and spotless sacrifices necessary at Christ's table. (See Jude 24.) *Reefs* is also possible and is in keeping with the shipwreck imagery that follows. Jude's opponents may sink the faith of his readers if believers are not careful. (See 1 Timothy 1:19.)

Feeding only themselves is a reference to shepherds who do not watch their flocks but only care about their own welfare. For *clouds* see Proverbs 25:14. *Fruitless trees* points to the Jewish tradition that the unfaithful cannot produce for God (see Matthew 7:16-20; Luke 6:43). For *wild waves* compare Isaiah 57:20. *Wandering stars* is from 1 Enoch, and is another term for angels who were believed in the ancient world to be in control of different levels of the heavens. Jude says that they are condemned to Hell (*blackest* [NIV; NRSV = *deepest*] *darkness*). Sometimes Jewish tradition described eternal punishment as fire, sometimes as darkness. Gloom is more appropriate here since the light of the stars will be put out when God judges them.

In verses 14-16 the author quotes from portions of 1 Enoch, especially 1:9. According to Genesis 5:21-24, Enoch was the seventh generation of human beings in Adam's line. Jewish tradition states that he was taken bodily to heaven and had many visions revealed to him by God. In the early church, particularly after all the books of the New Testament had been written, 1 Enoch was regarded as an inspired writing. Here Jude quotes a verse from that book to indicate that God will be coming soon in judgment, especially to punish the ungodly.

Grumblers and *malcontents* (NRSV; NIV = *faultfinders*) are references to the murmuring and complaining of the Israelites when God led them through the wilderness to the Promised Land (see Numbers 14:27-29). For flattering people see the comments on James 2:1-9. The reference in Jude 16 is to those who show partiality to the rich and influential while ignoring others who are poor and powerless.

Verses 17-23 provide a word of encouragement to those who do not follow the ungodly but remain faithful to God in Christ: They will be given mercy by God and will be kept in God's love. For predictions of the apostles see the discussions of 1 Peter 1:1 and 1:10. Although verse 18 looks like a quotation from the Scriptures, the source of the words cannot be identified. They are either from a text that is now lost or merely a reference to the general idea about the way unbelievers will be punished at the time of final judgment (see Matthew 24:21-28; Mark 13:19-23).

Scoffers is a term found only here and in 2 Peter 3:3 (see Isaiah 3:5); it identifies those who do not have the gifts of the Holy Spirit and make fun of believers who do. For *eternal life* see 1 John 1:1-4.

In verses 22-23 three different kinds of Christian backsliders are identified: doubters, those who are already in the fire, and people contaminated by the ungodly. Jude's readers are urged to try and help them. The Greek texts of these verses are very uncertain. However, the expression *snatch from the fire* appears to be a reference to Zechariah 3:1-5 or Amos 4:11, and the way God can rescue the people from destruction. Apparently some of Jude's readers were on the brink of Hell and needed other church members to save them at the last moment.

Clothing stained by corrupted flesh (NIV; NRSV = *tunic defiled by their bodies*) is probably connected with Zechariah 3:3-4. Faithful Christians can be contaminated by those who are sexually loose, just as they can get dirty from coming into contact with someone wearing filthy clothes. The advice in these verses is similar to that found elsewhere in the New Testament. (See the discussion of James 5:19-20.)

§ § § § § § §

The Message of Jude 5-23

The main section of Jude is concerned with giving a warning to believers about what happens to those who follow the behavior of the ungodly. A number of examples are given of heavenly and human individuals. In verses 17-23 encouragement is provided to those who hold fast. They will be kept in the love of God in Christ and by their own faithfulness will be able to save others from going to Hell.

§ § § § § § §

Jude 24-25

Introduction to These Verses

Jude closes with a beautiful benediction that is often used at the end of services of worship today. The word *doxology* comes from the Greek word for *glory* (*doxa*), which refers to God's weight or value. Doxologies give praise and honor to God, and often express faith when nothing more can be said. Other examples are found in Romans 9:5; 11:36; 2 Corinthians 1:20; Galatians 1:5; Ephesians 1:14.

Closing Doxology (verses 24-25)

Falling in verse 24 is found only here in the New Testament, and indicates that God can uphold those who believe in Christ no matter what happens to them. (See Psalms 38:16-22; 56:13; 2 Thessalonians 3:3.) *Without blemish* (NRSV; NIV = *fault*, compare verse 12) is a term borrowed from Jewish sacrificial language. Lambs offered to God had to be pure and spotless, and so Christ, the one who makes mercy possible through his cross, presents the faithful to God without any imperfection. (See Ephesians 1:4; 5:27; Colossians 1:22; 1 Thessalonians 3:13.)

The words *to the only God* clearly reflect the Jewish and Christian belief that there are not many gods but only one true God (Nehemiah 9:6; Psalms 83:18; 86:10; Romans 16:27; 1 Timothy 1:17). *Savior* is a term often applied to God in the Old Testament (Psalm 106:21; Isaiah 49:26).

Here, however, the word probably refers to Jesus (see Luke 2:11; John 4:42; Philippians 3:20).

Majesty describes the loftiness of God and Christ above all other beings, earthly or heavenly. *Authority* also means *power*, and implies that God in Christ has control over all creatures—even the angels, the devil, and heavenly beings called *authorities* or *powers* elsewhere in the New Testament (compare Ephesians 1:21-23). God's power is eternal. It is from the beginning, before there was any time, right through to the very end (*before all time and now and for ever*). *Amen* is a typical Jewish ending of a prayer, and means *be it so.*

§ § § § § § §

The Message of Jude 24-25

Jude ends with words of praise for God and Christ. God will keep true believers from falling from salvation. Through Christ God has power and authority over all creatures in heaven and on earth and for all eternity.

§ § § § § § §

Glossary of Terms

Abraham: The Old Testament hero whose story begins in Genesis 11:26. In the New Testament he is often considered a model of faith and action.

Anointing: In the Old Testament kings and priests were inaugurated by having expensive oil placed on their heads. The word *messiah* means *anointed one.* In the New Testament anointing may mean baptism or confirmation.

Antichrist: Another name for the devil or Satan. He is opposed to Jesus Christ.

Antichrists: People who follow the Antichrist.

Apocryphal: Books and writings that reveal the hidden plans of God. Often they deal with the end of time and the coming day of judgment.

Apostle: One who is sent by God. A special title of authority and power in the early church.

Babylon: A symbolic name for Rome, the capital city of the Roman Empire.

Cain: The son of Adam and Eve who murdered his brother. In Jewish and Christian writings he was a symbol of evil.

Demetrius: A pastor or layperson who supported the author of Third John.

Diotrephes: The opponent of John in 3 John 9-10.

Dispersion: In the Old Testament it refers to the situation of living in foreign areas outside of Israel and Judah. In the New Testament it can refer to spiritual and/or cultural exile and alienation.

Dominion: The power of God.

Double-minded: A term used in James to describe unfaithful people who said one thing and did another.

Elijah: One of the major Old Testament prophets whose story is told in 1 Kings 17–19; 21 and 2 Kings 1–2. He was expected to reappear at the coming of the messiah and was reported to be present with Moses at Jesus' transfiguration.

Epicureanism: A philosophy based on the teachings of Epicurus (342?-270 B.C.). It taught that the gods did not influence the universe or human behavior and that people should avoid pain and excess desire. Followers of Epicurus were often accused of being pleasure seekers.

Evil One: Another term for the devil or Satan.

Exhort: To offer moral advice or Christian teaching.

Expiation: The act of atoning or making payment for sin.

Fulness of time: Just the right time when God's plans will finally be realized.

Gaius: A church leader loyal to the author of 3 John (verses 5-8).

Gentiles: A word used by Jews to describe all non-Jews.

Glory: God's majesty. Literally it refers to one's weight or value.

Gnostic: A person who believed in Gnosticism.

Gnosticism: Philosophical systems and religions that placed great emphasis on special knowledge (*gnosis*) possessed by members. Gnostics often believed in complex systems of heavens on many different planes and divine beings that populated them.

Grace: The gift of God's love and forgiveness through Jesus Christ.

Hellenism: A name given to the Greek culture that influenced the ancient world following the death of Alexander the Great.

Isaac: The son born to Abraham and Sarah in their old age. His story is told in Genesis 17–35.

Job: The hero of the biblical book of Job. He was known for his great suffering, his patience, and his persistent faith in God.

Mystery: The secret of God's plan in Christ for both Jews and Gentiles. The New Testament writers believed that it was uncovered for the first time through Jesus' life, death, and resurrection. In the ancient world other religious groups believed that they were the only ones who were initiated into God's secrets and thus their belief systems were often called *mystery religions.*

Redemption: The act of exchanging one thing for something else. In the Bible it refers to God's payment for the high cost of sin. In the New Testament it refers to the sacrifice of Christ and the way it brings about God's forgiveness.

Repentance: A New Testament word for spiritual change of heart, which means *turning around* or *change of mind.*

Salvation: The process by which God rescues believers from sin. In the New Testament it comes through Jesus, his death on the cross, and his resurrection from the dead.

Sarah: The woman who laughed when God told her she would have a son in her old age. The mother of Isaac and wife of Abraham, she was often considered to be a model of true faith in Jewish and Christian tradition.

Sin: Rebellion or hostility directed toward God; literally "missing the mark."

World: This word has two different meanings in the New Testament. It can refer to the universe or *cosmos* God created or to the atmosphere of evil and sin that corrupts humanity.

Zion: A name for the fortress or citadel in Jerusalem. In the Bible it sometimes stands for God's kingdom on earth or God's rule in heaven that is yet to come.

Guide to Pronunciation

Antichrist: AN-tee-christ
Babylon: BAB-eh-lon
Balaam: BAY-lam
Beor: Beh-OR
Bithynia: Bih-THIN-ee-ah
Cappadocia: Cap-ah-DOSH-ee-ah
Demetrius: Deh-MEE-tree-us
Diotrephes: Die-AH-tref-ays
Elijah: Ee-LIGH-jah
Gaius: GAY-us
Galatia: Gah-LAY-shuh
Gentile: JEN-tile
Gnostic: NOS-tik
Gnosticism: NOS-ti-siz-um
Rahab: RAY-hab
Silvanus: Sill-VAY-nus
Zion: ZIGH-un

CPSIA inform
Printed in the
BVOW11s22
341268E

Atlanta-Fulton Public Library

26487